Pilgrimage

A Medieval Cure for Modern Ills

Dave Whitson

ABOUT THE AUTHOR

Dave Whitson is a teacher from Portland, Oregon, USA. He is the author of three guidebooks on different branches of the Camino de Santiago, published by Cicerone Press: *The Camino del Norte and Primitivo*, *The Camino Inglés and Ruta do Mar*, and *Walking the Camino de Santiago - Via Podiensis*. He also hosts The Camino Podcast.

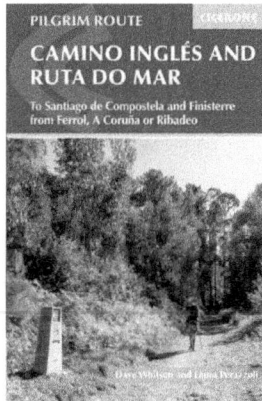

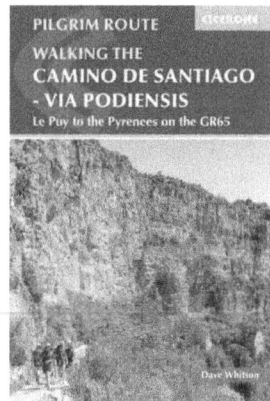

CONTENTS

ACKNOWLEDGMENTS

This book was written during peak COVID. All things considered, I was among the lucky during the pandemic. My family remained healthy and well, not to mention financially stable, and I had a less painful transition to online teaching than many of my colleagues.

That said, I didn't emerge entirely unscathed. When COVID shutdowns began, I was in Canaan Valley, West Virginia, some 2200 miles into my trans-USA walk on the American Discovery Trail. Less than a week later, I pulled the plug, grudgingly doing the responsible thing and heading home. This was discouraging.

Homebound for months, this book gave me purpose. And throughout the lengthy process of researching and writing this book, two people gave me crucial support and motivation. Catie Kean and Lauren Selden, two students who had previously walked on pilgrimage with me, journeyed with me through every step of this endeavor as well. This manuscript is as clean and lean as it is because of Catie's eagle-eyed and merciless copy-editing, while Lauren's enthusiasm for pilgrimage studies will only become more apparent in the years ahead, as she makes her own mark in the field.

I am also grateful to every pilgrim and scholar quoted in this text, many of whom also spoke with me on The Camino Podcast. It is only through their candor and openness, their disciplined expertise, and their generosity of spirit that I was better able to develop meaningful insight into my own pilgrimage experience, and the pilgrimage tradition more broadly. My sincere hope is that this book becomes a conduit for many readers to those authors' books, blogs, and articles, each of which deserves to be read in full.

A special word of thanks to Fritz Nordengren, Stephen Drew, and Sandy Brown, who reviewed an earlier draft of this manuscript and offered critical feedback and positive encouragement.

Finally, I'm grateful to all who choose to read this. There is no shortage of books on pilgrimage at this point, and I recognize that this strays quite a bit from convention. I hope you get something from it. Please get in touch if anything here resonates with your own journey: caminopodcast@gmail.com.

Dave Whitson
December 2022

INTRODUCTION

My first pilgrimage ended in pain. Frankly, it started in pain, too. I suppose, if we're being honest here, that pain was a constant travel companion throughout the journey.

Nearly twenty years removed from that first walk on the Camino de Santiago through Spain, the memories remain vivid. Despite being in my early twenties, I was hardly fit. On the first day's climb over the Pyrenees, mere kilometers into the ascent, I collapsed onto a rock as my quads spasmed uncontrollably. Other pilgrims slowed in concern as they walked by. Days later, my knees seized the spotlight, trumpeting their grievances so abrasively that I paused atop a steep descent for minutes, pondering whether it would hurt less to simply roll to the bottom.

Moving into the final stages, the discomfort migrated upward to my shoulders, which throbbed when jostled, even slightly. Unfortunately, shoulders are rather important when backpacking. Not wanting to endure the agony any more than necessary, I pushed through the final 40km in a single go, never once removing my backpack until I staggered into my hotel in Santiago de Compostela, collapsing into a bed and not moving for hours, aside from the whimpers.

As I lay dying—my imminent death, it turns out, was a bit of whiny hyperbole—I had one coherent thought running through my mind: when can I come back and do this again?

$$*\qquad*\qquad*\qquad*\qquad*$$

Flying home to the USA, a second thought took over: how on earth will I explain this to others back home? Heck, I couldn't even fully explain it to myself! Growing up in the Pacific Northwest, I developed into an insufferable atheist, so a religious pilgrimage seemed like an odd fit. I certainly did not crave highly sociable environments; even as a young traveler in Europe, my introversion pushed me toward private rooms instead of hostels, much to the consternation of my budget. I wasn't much of an outdoorsman, either. Even after spending a month on pilgrimage, it was challenging to articulate what drove me to it, let alone what was already pulling me back. Unlike today, few in the USA knew about the Camino de Santiago, so the concept was foreign to everyone in my life. I muddled through the same uncertain terrain in every conversation, over and over, in the weeks following my return.

My uneasiness was hardly atypical. While pilgrims certainly look forward to homecomings with loved ones, that excitement is often tempered with the challenge of translating a profound and protean experience into mundane and concrete language.

I knew that something exceptional had happened, something that was both discrete and ongoing, something that would fundamentally reshape my life moving forward. While I couldn't appreciate the full magnitude of the impact then, much of my adult life has indeed been permeated by pilgrimage. I lead groups of my high school students on walking pilgrimages most summers. I've written guidebooks on branches of the Camino de Santiago for Cicerone Press. And, sporadically, I've produced a podcast on pilgrimage, the Camino Podcast, that has allowed me to connect with pilgrims and other relevant experts around the world.

I've walked thousands and thousands of miles on pilgrim roads over these past two decades, toward Santiago de Compostela and Rome, Canterbury and Trondheim, Jerusalem and Kumano Hongu Taisha. I've felt the Ganges course through my fingers, watched the faithful bathe in the Haridwar ghats, and climbed the holy mountains of Wutai Shan and Olympus. I've stood beneath towering cathedral spires and within silent, towering woods, been surrounded by the dead of Okunoin in Koyasan and the living in the candlelight procession at Lourdes, witnessed the black virgins of Le Puy-en-Velay and Rocamadour and Czestochowa, touched the largest surviving piece of the True Cross in Santo Toribio, sought guidance from the oracle at Delphi, and watched the sun set at the world's end.

For all the awe and wonder generated by these places of natural splendor, human creativity and ingenuity, and shared belief, I've also marveled at my own growing capacity. On the tenth day of that first pilgrimage, for reasons as unclear today as they were at the time, I pushed myself much farther than I'd ever gone before, walking 35 kilometers (around 21 miles) to Villafranca Montes de Oca. I was exhausted, completely spent. I found a room for rent in a truck-stop motel; food options were poor, so I settled for a bag of *magdalenas* (Spanish muffins) from a hole-in-the-wall bakery. I flopped onto the venerable bed in the spartan room, with the gradually emptying muffin bag perched on my stomach, and proceeded to stare vacantly at the ceiling for the remainder of the afternoon. In that moment, too, I felt awe—awe at what I had done, what I was doing, and what I could continue to do in the days and weeks ahead.

Like a pilgrim to Lourdes that you'll hear from later, I wouldn't claim that this has transformed me into a completely different person. I'm now a tolerant agnostic, generally secular in outlook, and still a steadfast introvert. I'm definitely a much stronger walker.

Nonetheless, I've never stopped struggling with inquiries from people about why I continue to go on pilgrimage, why I feel this inexplicable certainty about its importance in my life. Instead, I've just become more skilled at evading the question and changing the subject.

*   *   *   *   *

I've come to realize that one of the major reasons that it's challenging to pin down the source of my ongoing motivations to participate in pilgrimage is that the experience is multi-faceted. If you're seeking treatment for your back, you go to a chiropractor; if you're suffering from tooth pain, you'll head to the dentist (after putting it off for as long as possible). The desire to go on pilgrimage, however, speaks to many different needs. Countless pilgrims embark hoping to treat a known symptom, only to find relief for a much deeper, underlying condition.

We also happen to be living in a moment when pilgrimage speaks to particularly acute deficits and difficulties. We are sedentary shut-ins, increasingly favoring artificial online connectivity over the in-person communities that are far more enriching. Shut off from nature, stripped of clarity of purpose, and constantly distracted, many of us struggle to find the spark in life that gives it meaning and joy.

We are, in short, disconnected. Or, sometimes even worse, confoundingly mis-connected.

In this book, I hope to share how pilgrimage can reconnect us to the physical world, our deeper selves, other people, and spiritual belief, and in so doing help reforge a link with the sources of so many good things in our lives, like health, joy, inspiration, peace, and meaning. To accomplish this, I've assembled a wealth of perspectives. This book is not a single pilgrim's story; my personal experiences mostly sit on the margins of this narrative. Instead, I synthesize academic research on both the challenges we face and the many discrete elements that constitute pilgrimage, and then weave that together with excerpted anecdotes from many different pilgrims. Most writing on pilgrimage tends to operate solely in the realm of personal memoir or academic study; by bridging that gap, this book strives to use those sources as complementary perspectives, each lending insight to the other. The wisdom of crowds trumps any individual's expertise.

My goal is for this book to be of service to several distinct audiences. First and foremost, I hope that it speaks to other experienced pilgrims, offering insight and clarity into their lived experience. Even after twenty years of pilgrimage, this research project was still instructive for me in laying bare some of what I had encountered but never fully recognized. Second, I aim for this book to be a resource for friends and family of pilgrims, to help reveal what their loved ones are pursuing and why, and thus set the table for a richer series of conversations upon their return.

Finally, I aspire for this book to be a source of inspiration for those who have never gone on pilgrimage, or even considered the notion. Most pilgrims that I know found their way to the practice by accident or coincidence. They stumbled across a television program or movie that offered inspiration, or they happened to drop by a presentation at their outdoor store or church, or one website led to another and... there they were. Once they encountered the idea, though, something clicked. A bell rang that simply couldn't be unrung. For whatever reason, for a million reasons, they immediately recognized that there was something for them here. I think there's something for you here, too.

*   *   *   *   *

I should pause at this point to address a thorny question: what, *exactly*, is a pilgrimage?

There is no shortage of possible answers coming from the realm of academia. Here are three: Alan Morinis (1992) defines pilgrimage as "a journey undertaken by a person in quest of a place or a state that he or she believes to embody a valued ideal."[1] Luigi Tomasi (2002), meanwhile, characterizes it as "a journey undertaken for religious purposes that culminates in a visit to a place considered to be the site or manifestation of the supernatural—a place where it is easier to obtain divine help."[2] Finally, Richard Barber (1993) offers the following: "a journey resulting from religious causes, externally to a holy site, and internally for spiritual purposes and internal understanding."[3]

Some patterns emerge from those three definitions. Pilgrimage is a journey toward *something*. A spiritual or religious influence is at play, providing the impetus to depart or a sacred destination to strive for, though Morinis's language—"a valued ideal"—is more flexible. That said, it's hard not to feel unsatisfied by these offerings, given their general vagueness.

One of the major challenges that impedes the development of a less... mushy definition of pilgrimage is that the act encompasses a wide array of practices. In acknowledgement of that, Morinis also developed a typology of pilgrimage, laying out six different kinds. *Devotional pilgrimages*, like the Camino de Santiago historically, offer the possibility to encounter the divine and a chance to earn merit. *Instrumental pilgrimages*, meanwhile, serve very specific, worldly goals, in the way that pilgrims to Lourdes, France might pray for a miracle cure for a dire illness. The third category, *normative pilgrimages*, are annual traditions, often linked to seasonal moments, or journeys pegged to specific moments in a person's life, like elderly pilgrims traveling to Banaras, India.

Obligatory pilgrimages are an obvious fit for the Hajj to Mecca, but this also includes pilgrimages that are assigned as punishment, providing an opportunity for penance. Solitary seekers and Zen pilgrims might pursue a *wandering pilgrimage*; my first experience on the Via Francigena, getting lost constantly, does not qualify. Finally, Morinis highlights *initiatory pilgrimages*, rites of passage in which the subject transitions into a new stage of life.

Pilgrims are often defined in opposition. Sure, it might be hard to pin down exactly what they are, but we know exactly what they aren't: tourists. Catch a group of pilgrims on a bad day and you'll hear all about the sins perpetrated by tourists—their shallow hedonism, their softness, their inauthenticity. It's fascinating, though, to look more closely at that label, tourist. As Tomasi explains, it arose in 16th century Europe and proliferated over the next two centuries. Whereas travel had previously been arduous and often unpleasant—hence the link between travel and travail—the rise of hotels and other creature comforts took the edge off the experience. More consequentially, it became normalized and intentional; the "Grand Tour" offered an itinerary that promised education and cultural refinement, visiting Europe's renowned architectural and artistic works. A tourist, in that age, was simply one who completed that circuit—a physical journey that promised internal growth.

That returns us to Barber's definition, which stresses the dual journeys, within and without, which I find to be the most instructive way of thinking about pilgrimage. It also aligns with the thinking of Victor Turner, the forefather of pilgrimage studies, who famously wrote that "if a tourist is half pilgrim, a pilgrim is half tourist."[4]

*   *   *   *   *

While my experience is grounded in walking pilgrimages, I have strived to synthesize research and stories from a much wider array of perspectives in this book. You'll encounter more than two dozen different pilgrimages in these pages, with representative examples of five of Morinis's six types (my apologies to the wanderers). These are all described in further detail in the appendix. One of the most striking discoveries that I made as I navigated the available materials on different sacred destinations is how many consistent qualities were made manifest across highly distinct places and contexts. I'm not foolish enough to claim that any of these are universal, cutting across *every* pilgrimage, but there is sufficient commonality to take note.

That said, a significant portion of the book draws from walking pilgrimages—not just the Camino de Santiago, but also the Via Francigena to Rome, the Abraham Path in the Middle East, and the 88 Temples of Shikoku, among many others. This is driven in part by the abundance of written accounts that exist from these routes. The growing popularity of walking pilgrimages in recent decades has been accompanied by a proliferation of pilgrim memoirs, and these are often rich sources of insight. It doesn't hurt that walking pilgrimages are often—though not always— longer in duration, and therefore provide greater opportunity for personal reflection and transformation.

Otherwise, I have mostly—with one glaring exception—adhered to a rather traditional definition of pilgrimage when choosing case studies, focusing primarily on sites associated with the major world religions. You won't find Graceland in these pages, nor Burning Man, nor any of the other secular pilgrimages that have loyal contingents associated with them. This is not a value judgement. Rather, it's an attempt to keep a fairly amorphous subject more closely circumscribed. I suspect, though, that the insights offered in these pages could have broader relevance to those varied contexts.

Finally, in assembling academic research for the following pages, I have selected a small set of representative studies that reflect broader trends in the literature. When possible, I spotlight meta-analyses, studies that synthesize a wider array of research and offer more generalizable conclusions. There is always some risk when operating outside of the realm of one's disciplinary expertise; in the effort to avoid misrepresenting important findings or muddling the intent behind precise language, I include a number of direct quotations and also list all selected studies in the endnotes. Many of these topics are emerging fields of study, with fresh research deepening and refining our understanding seemingly every month, so I encourage readers to review recent updates.

*   *   *   *   *

Despite what the title claims, I recognize that pilgrimage can't fix *all* of the problems we face today. It can't bring down oppressive regimes, nor can it resolve growing income inequality. It was powerless in the face of the coronavirus and won't be of any help with climate change. It can't eliminate racial bigotry any more than it can feed the hungry.

It *can*, however, provide an opportunity to break away from many of the corrosive aspects of contemporary culture, to immerse ourselves in a healthier and more optimistic setting, and to recast our own personal narratives, enabling us to find a deeper purpose and greater meaning. It can reconnect us with what really matters.

The following pages will tell you how.

OPENING THE DOOR

Imagine a pilgrimage site. What comes to mind? For many in the west, I suspect your thoughts might veer swiftly towards religious edifices—the Vatican, the Church of the Holy Sepulchre in Jerusalem, the Marian shrine in Lourdes, or the Kaaba in Mecca. And those are all legitimate, but they also risk distilling the pilgrimage experience down to a simple act of worshipping inside.

On the contrary, two of the great boons of pilgrimage involve how the experience often immerses us in natural splendor and sets us in motion, boons needed more urgently today than perhaps ever before in human history. As memorable as the cathedral in Santiago de Compostela may be, for many pilgrims on the Camino de Santiago the most revelatory experiences take place along the trail—crossing the Pyrenees, amidst the barren sprawl of the *meseta*, in the dramatic descent from O Cebreiro.

Many complex, nuanced strategies exist to improve our quality of life in contemporary society and some of those certainly merit attention. However, two of the most effective and proven methods are as simple and straightforward as could be. When we venture outside and experience the world on foot more regularly, we better position ourselves for encounters with awe and beauty, and we open the door to becoming healthier and happier people.

*   *   *   *   *

Modern human life can be summed up in three words: we sit inside. And those three words capture two alarming public health phenomena. First, we tend toward overwhelmingly sedentary lifestyles. On average, people in developed countries walk some 16km less on a daily basis than peers in non-motorized regions (Lunga 2006, Jorgenson 2008).[1] We replace that movement with sitting—a *lot* of sitting. The World Health Organization (WHO) has identified physical inactivity as a "Global Public Health Problem," noting that around 31% of adults 15 and over engaged in insufficient physical activity in 2008.[2] Americans are particularly prolific sitters; roughly 43% qualify as sedentary, the largest share in the world (Mitten et al 2016).[3]

That inactivity is killing us. Dr. James Levine, the director of the Mayo Clinic at Arizona State University, raised eyebrows in 2012 when he declared sitting to be the new smoking, but if a little hyperbole can be forgiven the assertion otherwise has validity.[4] In their survey of available literature on the state of human immobility in 2016, Denise Mitten and colleagues determined that chronic inactivity "accounts for an estimated 6% to 10% of all deaths from major noncommunicable diseases and 9% of premature deaths worldwide." A meta-analysis conducted by Leandro Fornias Machado de Rezende and colleagues in 2014 that reviewed 27 published articles on the health consequences of a sedentary lifestyle also paints a stark picture.[5] The researchers found a significant positive association between sedentary behavior—defined in these studies as two or more hours of screen/sitting time—and cardiovascular disease, *regardless* of the accompanying level of physical activity. Similarly, sedentary behavior has also been found to share a positive association with type 2 diabetes in adults—again, *regardless* of physical activity level. Notably, groundbreaking work completed by Susan C. Gilchrist and colleagues in 2020 established a definitive relationship between immobility and cancer death.[6] In Gilchrist's words, "Our findings show that the amount of time a person spends sitting prior to a cancer diagnosis is predictive of time to cancer death."[7] The new smoking, indeed.

The consequences of these passive pastimes are abundantly evident. As the WHO has documented, global obesity has, at least, tripled since 1975. In 2016, 39% of adults were overweight, while 13% were obese.[8] Perhaps more alarming, over 340 million children and adolescents were overweight or obese as well. The European Union (22% obesity rate) is healthier than the USA (36%), with other developed countries falling in between those poles, but the trend holds true across the board. As Penny Gordon-Larsen and colleagues summarized in 2009, "Many studies have reported a decreased physical activity and an increased prevalence of overweight/obesity across all sex, age, and race/ethnic groups examined in the past 2 decades."[9] This has wide-ranging health implications, but to offer just one: the global prevalence of diabetes has skyrocketed over the same time period, with the WHO noting an increase from 4.7% of adults in 1980 to 8.5% in 2014. In the USA, 34.1 million adults, or 13% of all American adults, had diabetes in 2018, while some 88 million other adults had prediabetes. Once again, while the USA leads the way, its peer countries are also trending in the wrong direction.

While it's easy to focus on the physical consequences of inactivity, the ripple effect is far greater. As Yannick Stephan and colleagues documented in 2018, a sedentary lifestyle leads to declines in three of the "big five" personality traits: openness, extraversion, and agreeableness.[10] The authors acknowledge that more research needs to be done, but they conclude that their study "provides some initial evidence that physical inactivity is related to long-term personality change."

Of course, to this point we've only focused on the first of those two public health phenomena introduced above. We don't just sit; we sit *inside*. The trends are remarkably consistent across developed countries. According to an EPA study, Americans spend 93% of their time in built environments—87% in buildings and a further 6% in cars.[11] Meanwhile, the European Commission at its Joint Research Centre determined that Europeans spend 90% of their time inside.[12] And we have only just started to fully reckon with the wide-ranging consequences of this tendency over the last two decades.

*   *   *   *   *

Edie Littlefield Sundby was living her best life.[13] An active and energetic 55-year-old, she enjoyed everything that lovely San Diego, California had to offer. In her own words, she was "arrogantly healthy and joyously happy." She had a thriving professional life, collaborating with her devoted husband on exciting new initiatives, and four daughters who were gracefully easing into adulthood. She had everything to live for.

But then her doctor dropped the bomb: "You have cancer, lots of it." As if a seventeen-centimeter solid mass wasn't bleak enough, the cancer originated in her gallbladder, challenging to diagnose and daunting to survive. Edie went from seemingly healthy to stage 4 in a conversation. She had less than a 2% chance of lasting five years; the median survival length for advanced gallbladder cancer was a meager two to four months.

What can one do in the aftermath of such a life-altering revelation? Alone, Edie staggered to her car, somehow putting the machine in motion. Before long, though, she pulled over, parking under a tree and an old mission bell. In that moment, as she first confronted this heart-wrenching new reality, she took note of the world around her: "The morning was sunny with a gentle breeze. It was peaceful under the tree, quiet, with the soft rustle of wind moving the leaves. A narrow beam of sunlight flickered through the branches above the mission bell and into the open car window, and its warmth relaxed my clenched jaw. How could I die and leave this?"

The fight was on.

$$* \quad * \quad * \quad * \quad *$$

Why did Edie feel so peaceful beneath that tree? Research from Japan offers a clue.

In *Forest Bathing: How Trees Can Help You Find Health and Happiness*, Dr. Qing Li describes the Japanese phenomenon of shinrin-yoku, or forest bathing.[14] Qing, the founding member and chairman of the Japanese Society for Forest Medicine, has been at the forefront of groundbreaking research into the health benefits of this practice over the past two decades.

As he explains, Japan is a forest civilization, and "both of its official religions—Shinto and Buddhism—believe that the forest is the realm of the divine." Whereas western thought often frames a dichotomy between humans and nature, in Japanese culture the two are interwoven. In Zen aesthetics, the principle of "shizen" or "naturalness," captures the idea that "we are all connected to nature, emotionally, spiritually and physically" and "the more closely something relates to nature, the more pleasing it is."

Despite its forest ties, Japanese life is increasingly urban, with 78% of Japanese people now living in cities. While that outpaces global numbers, the upward trend is universal. In 2016, UN estimates placed four billion people, or 54% of humanity, in cities. Concerned about this growing distance from nature, a national health program was introduced in Japan in 1982 to promote forest bathing, based largely on the intuition that it would be beneficial.

That intuition has been decisively validated. Through the research of Qing and many others, we now have evidence that forest bathing—which Qing describes as "taking in the forest through our senses"—can boost the immune system, most notably through the enhancement of natural killer cell activity, which may have an anti-cancer effect. As Komori and colleagues describe, spending time in a forest also has stress reduction effects, as it decreases the pulse rate, reduces cortisol, suppresses sympathetic activity, increases parasympathetic activity, and lowers blood pressure.

One of the more fascinating aspects of Qing's work is his study of phytoncides, the natural oils released by trees as part of their self-defense system. Qing describes how two nurses at Vanderbilt University Medical Center, concerned about the high-stress nature of their department, decided to experiment with the diffusion of essential oils, building off his research. The outcomes were dramatic: 41% of staff self-reported work-related stress before the use of essential oils, but only 3% did afterward. Conversely, where 13% of the staff felt equipped to manage stressful conditions before, this surged to 58% after. Additionally, self-assessed energy levels more than doubled, from 33 to 77%.

Those outcomes highlight an important aspect of forest bathing. While *some* walking is included in these studies, researchers are careful to restrict the movement to a typical daily limit. As we'll see, physical activity is a good thing, and it can amplify the benefits of being in a natural setting. However, the mere act of being immersed in the woods is healing, in and of itself.

*   *   *   *   *

Pilgrims, drawn to a sacred destination, often also feel the allure of nature. In her groundbreaking anthropological study, *Pilgrim Stories: On and Off the Road to Santiago*, Nancy Louise Frey developed deep insights into the experiences of walking pilgrims on Spain's Camino de Santiago in the 1990s.[15] While Frey encountered a wide range of different underlying motivations that inspired pilgrims on the Camino, she notes that, "The most common motivation was a longing for nature and outdoor life. Pilgrimages seem to have a function as a facilitator for people to get out to the forest or other scenic places."

One can see in these pilgrims' reflections many of the same forces at work in Japan's forests. Being in nature offers a break from modern disruptions, and consequently pilgrims' "perceptions of time and place are radically altered." This results in a "heightening of the senses," a sentiment that aligns with Qing's observation that we tend to employ only two senses in offices—sight and sound—whereas nature activates all five. This is a critical part of a larger unlocking process; through this contact with nature, "pilgrims often open themselves to potential personal and social transformation" and in the process their "journey becomes meaningful."

In his pilgrimage memoir, *El Camino: Walking to Santiago de Compostela*, Lee Hoinacki, a former Dominican priest and political science professor, describes this phenomenon vividly.[16] Early in his walk, he couldn't quite escape modernity, observing that "below me on the right, a hundred or more meters away, a highway runs parallel to the *camino*. Now and then, the vegetation is low enough that I can see the traffic. It seems to whiz by effortlessly, covering great distances rapidly, while for me every step is slow and awkward." If Hoinacki seems to bemoan his transportation choice in that passage, he quickly turned the table. A driver, he notes, "can be almost anesthetized," while Hoinacki moved "in a heightened state of consciousness, alert to many aspects of my surroundings at every instant."

That "heightening" is on full display in Hoinacki's narrative. Even as he slogged through mud, he still found each and every step to be "a distinct and separate act, a new adventure." There was neither tedium nor drudgery here; on the contrary, the walk offered "a particular and special grace." He looked up from his feet and observed that "I move only through beauty." It was not, however, a conventional beauty. Rather, the "particularity of each place [added] up to an infinitude of *different* places." Only by virtue of walking slowly, immersed in nature, did Hoinacki "see particularity," or "sense a uniqueness that stretches out forever."

*   *   *   *   *

Trees alone don't claim a monopoly on healing power; nature's potency is well documented in all its varied forms.

Some of the most noteworthy findings involve people who are physically prevented from going outside. Roger Ulrich examined 46 patients in a suburban Pennsylvania hospital over the course of a decade, half of whom had a view of a tree, half of whom could only see a brick wall.[17] As Ulrich concludes, "the patients with the tree view had shorter postoperative hospital stays, had fewer negative evaluative comments from nurses, took fewer moderate and strong analgesic doses, and had slightly lower scores for minor postsurgical complications." Seong-Hyun Park and Richard Mattson built on this work, by adding natural elements into the hospital room—specifically live, ornamental plants.[18] The findings were, once again, quite encouraging—patients staying in those rooms exhibited lower systolic blood pressure, reported less pain, anxiety, and fatigue, and felt more positive about both the room and the hospital staff. Simply *seeing* nature, whether from a distance or in a domesticated context, made patients healthier.

Of course, it's better to be *in* nature. As Qing noted, our increasingly urban lives are often made more stressful by both the separation from nature and the bustle and strains of cities. Can a short break in a natural setting—*any* natural setting—help to restore some of the damage done? Mathew P. White and colleagues set out to explore this question, focusing on the four components of restoration: feeling calm, relaxed, revitalized, and refreshed.[19] Their study examined a large sample of roughly 4300 participants who had visited a natural environment within the past week and self-reported some feeling cure of restoration. They discovered that there is, essentially, a sliding scale of benefit; urban parks offer a modest benefit to restoration, while more spectacular settings like coasts and mountains offer more robust rewards. Visit duration and age also matter; longer trips bring greater restoration and older participants reported more significant gains. Nature has a restorative effect, but some contexts and conditions are more rejuvenating than others.

Much of the research on the health benefits of nature are limited by the short time periods observed in published studies. Ian Alcock and his colleagues set out to rectify this with a longitudinal study, tracking a group of more than 1000 British participants over the course of five years.[20] This sample was composed of people who moved between the second and third year of the study and were already contributors to the British Household Panel Survey, which included mental health data. Alcock and his colleagues cleverly determined whether participants moved toward greener areas or away from them and then tracked whether their mental health improved over that time. The outcome is striking. When the grass was literally greener on the other side, it was figuratively so as well—a move to greener urban areas aligned with appreciably improved mental health over the course of all three years. This is, perhaps, even more notable than it sounds. Many important changes in life circumstances result in only a temporary shift in mental health; we have a remarkably persistent pull to our baseline. In this case, however, the positive change persisted across multiple years.

While most of the discussion to this point has centered on the personal benefits of exposure to nature, a growing body of research highlights its prosocial benefits as well. That is to say, when we see and appreciate nature, we have a greater tendency to be oriented towards helping others or society more broadly. Jia Wei Zhang and colleagues have demonstrated that people exposed to more beautiful images of nature—just pictures!—become more generous and trusting as a consequence.[21] Similarly, study participants exposed to more beautiful plants in the laboratory responded by demonstrating more helpful behavior.

As with the hospital patients discussed above, the most superficial representations of nature spur positive outcomes. Why is this the case? Zhang and colleagues speculate that, on the most basic level, it's because nature makes us feel good. Numerous studies have identified a correlation between positive emotions and presence in nature, but George MacKerron and Susana Mourato deserve special attention for their ingenuity.[22] They developed a smartphone app that periodically prompted participants to report their happiness in that moment on a sliding scale. The app also tracked GPS data, allowing the researchers to track the degree to which those happiness scores correlated with the subjects' geographic location. After controlling for all kinds of factors—things like weather, daylight, activity, companionship, and location type—MacKerron and Mourato found that "study participants are significantly and substantially happier outdoors in all green or natural habitat types than they are in urban environments."

It's just that simple: we're happier in nature, regardless of what we're doing while we're there.

*   *   *   *   *

Nature is not only peaceful, pleasant, and beautiful; it is also inextricably associated with the divine. Mountains and rivers, in particular, carry sacred connotations across many cultures. In India, these stand out as common pilgrimage destinations, especially Ganga Ma, or the Ganges River. As Diane Eck explains in her magisterial work, *Banaras: City of Light,* the Ganges is sacred and revered, believed to have fallen directly from heaven to earth.[23] A similar scene is conducted all along its course: "Hindus bathe in the Ganges. They take up her water cupped in their hands and pour it back into the river as an offering to ancestors and the Gods. They present to the river, as to a deity, offerings of flowers and small clay oilwick lamps." The Ganges is goddess and mother. In Roger Housden's words, "She is the unequivocal fountain of mercy and compassion, here in this world only to comfort her children. Her waters are the milk, the nectar, of immortality, source of all life and abundance."[24]

The closest word to "pilgrimage" in Hindi is "tirthayatra," which literally translates as "journeys to river fords." Meanwhile, the anthropologist Ann Grodzins Gold describes Indian pilgrimage as "a turning from involvement in the world," or a renunciation, a temporary version of the ultimate turning away offered by moksha.[25] E.V. Daniel, carries this further, highlighting the habit of "modern pilgrims shedding birth-given identities," and thus transforming themselves into something new and different.[26] As such, Hindu pilgrimage is journey and destination, culmination and new beginning, crossing over and breaking off.

And Banaras, or Varanasi as it is also known, is the greatest of those fords on the Ganges. There is no more desirable place to die, given the prevailing belief that those cremated in Banaras—with their ashes subsequently released into the Ganges—will be freed from the reincarnation cycle. It also offers great promise, though, as a place to start anew. As Eck describes, "So great is the power of the Ganges to destroy sins that, it is said, even a droplet of Ganges water carried one's way by the breeze will erase the sins of many lifetimes in an instant." This is no mere symbolism. In Surinder Mohan Bhardwaj's words, when pilgrims bathe in the *amrita,* in this life-giving water, "a whole cosmic event is being reenacted;" the "myth is actualized, at the specific time and at the specific place." In the same way that a ford offers passage across a river, so too do tirthayatras link the numinous and mundane, bridging the gap between myth and reality.[27]

Rosemary Mahoney traveled the world to better understand modern pilgrims, visiting six sacred destinations. In Varanasi, she observed crowds of pilgrims at sunrise, lining the *ghats* (flights of broad steps) along the Ganges.[28] She watched them with envy, struggling with her own inability to pray. She had tried, sitting in the privacy of her hotel room, but she observed that "I was impatient and hasty, easily frustrated and reluctant to accept things as they were." And yet, she witnessed the Hindu faithful floating easily in the Ganges. "They looked entranced. Their gestures of prayer were delicate and small, and their bare brown shoulders glowed like pears in the early sunlight." After struggling with so many aspects of life in Varanasi—the sprawling waste, the appalling poverty, the overwhelming swell of humanity—Rosemary found the sacred here. "The praying pilgrims struck me as the most beautiful thing in Varanasi. The sight of so many calm people standing half naked in the river accentuated both the frailty and the grace of the human body."

Even in the midst of a city—in Housden's words, "one of the maddest, holiest, ugliest, most entrancing cities on earth"—these pilgrims found the calm Mahoney had lacked, by simply giving themselves to the river.

*   *   *   *   *

For all the promise of exposure to nature, passive measures are insufficient to single-handedly remedy the many physical and emotional challenges described at the beginning of this chapter. We have to shake the sedentary self and break away from the tyranny of screens, if we are to recover our collective health.

Despite the obscene proliferation of self-improvement programs and miracle cures on display across all advertising platforms and the overwhelming array of exercise equipment in cavernous fitness centers, increasing evidence suggests that one of the most reliable activities for personal health improvement is also the most venerable: walking.

*   *   *   *   *

Now in battle mode, Edie and her husband Dale mobilized their resources to move heaven and earth in pursuit of a cure. Their initial efforts proved discouraging. The message her husband received when Edie received a liver biopsy was, "Go home and prepare to die." She was more magnanimous in reflecting on this than one might imagine, acknowledging that palliative care was the best option for many in her situation, given the odds. Instead, Edie fought her way to the Stanford Cancer Center, where she started a regimen of chemotherapy. Reading Lance Armstrong's biography, she arrived at a profound insight: *"if you can move, you're not sick."* This proved pivotal in Edie's treatment, as she "decided right then and there that no matter what cancer did to me, I would continue to move. Movement was what the physical body was designed to do; it was how it coped and functioned. Movement was vitality. It was life. I would move. Always. No matter what. Until my last breath, I would move."

The chemotherapy continued to ravage Edie's body. In time, she was cleared for surgery, getting her gallbladder and 60% of her liver removed. Less than twenty-four hours later, she was out walking again. Chemotherapy resumed. Edie pressed on: "I refused to stop walking, even if just around the block. Walking was my connection with life. Regardless of what was happening inside, if I could get outside and walk, I felt better, and I didn't feel sick. And in this way, I survived four more months of chemotherapy."

To recharge, Edie and Dale traveled to Alaska and spent two weeks in the wilderness. They hiked, they canoed, they were surrounded by wildlife. Edie was freed, however briefly, from her burdens: "It was an altered state of mind, a journey without a destination. I was completely lost in nature and didn't care what day of the week it was."

Returning home, Edie kept walking. And as she did, the experience of walking began to transcend the physical: "I felt healing grace wash through my body and cleanse the tumors from my liver and lungs. I became a walking prayer."

Five years passed; already, Edie was the rarest of exceptions to the unforgiving odds. Even more encouraging, PET and CT scans revealed that her liver was now cancer-free. This result would allow Edie to move forward with lung surgery and hopefully remove the last cancerous enclave in her body.

Once again, Edie found herself sitting in her car, processing medical results while taking in the natural beauty around her. Once again, an old mission bell loomed overhead. This time, however, she registered that sight and it sparked her curiosity: "I wondered who put it there, and why." For the moment, though, it was just a passing thought.

*   *   *   *   *

While walking may be the oldest fitness regimen, the research on its effectiveness is surprisingly young. Only in the 1990s did a shift occur in public health discourse from promoting more vigorous activities like running toward more moderate practices like walking.[29] It's easy to be dismissive: running is exercise, the thinking goes, while walking is something one does to connect the couch and refrigerator. However, for able-bodied people, walking is essentially a universal practice, one with practically no entry-level requirements. There are ways to elevate the challenge involved, elongating the distances covered, pursuing more challenging terrain, and escalating the pace, but it's otherwise highly accessible. This is important when trying to start a new, healthier habit!

No single practice, of course, can undo the litany of negative health trends described at the beginning of this chapter, but the emerging research is clear: we can literally walk back some of them. We'll start with the physical. Walking promotes long-term weight change. In a 15-year longitudinal study conducted by Penny Gordon-Larsen and colleagues, the researchers tracked nearly 5,000 young American men and women, monitoring both their weight over time and their varied forms of physical activity.[30] Their work revealed that "an increase in walking over the early to middle adult years was associated with less weight gain over time and an increased likelihood of weight loss and maintenance compared with weight gain."

Weight gain is correlated with increased risk of diabetes, and a growing body of literature demonstrates the benefits of walking on that front as well. Carl Caspersen and Janet Fulton surveyed the available research in 2008 and reported some remarkably encouraging, if stark, findings.[31] Depending upon the data sets reviewed, they concluded that anywhere between 2 and 7 hours of walking per week could result in reductions in mortality between 40 and 55%. Even a half-hour of walking daily would place a person squarely in the midst of that admittedly broad range, increasing their odds considerably. With regards to diabetes specifically, the Diabetes Prevention Project conducted a trial in which at-risk participants went through a lifestyle intervention that included 150 minutes per week of brisk walking. That alone "reduced the risk of advancing from glucose intolerance to diabetes by over 50%."[32]

That word, "brisk," brings up an important point: pace can matter. Certainly, any walking is better than no walking. However, Caspersen and Fulton note that fast-paced walking could elevate reductions in mortality as far as 76%.

But wait, there's more! Walking appears to reduce breast cancer risk. Regan Howard and colleagues conducted a study of more than 45,000 women in order to gauge how different forms and levels of physical activity might influence the development of breast cancer.[33] They found that "the greatest risk reduction was among women who reported walking/hiking more than 10 hours per week, compared with those reporting no walking/hiking." Meanwhile, a study conducted of over 72,000 women demonstrated that walking related to a decreased risk of strokes, and particularly of ischemic strokes. As above, pace played a part; brisk walking offered additional benefit.[34]

While some might be concerned with the growing risk of falls for elderly participating in walks, the opposite appears to be true: a meta-analysis of four relevant studies of physical health interventions that included walking documented a 44% decrease in fall injuries.[35]

The list goes on. Study after study highlights the sustained, lasting benefits of a regular commitment to just putting one foot in front of the other.

* * * * *

While walking one day near his hometown of Morris, Connecticut, Stephen Drew experienced something transcendent. There he was, just putting one foot in front of the other. "One foot lifts up," he tells me, "and before it finds its way to the ground again, the entirety of the experience of walking the Camino de Santiago enters my life as a complete reality."[36] While Stephen had prior knowledge of the Camino, he had never explicitly considered making the trek. Suddenly, out of nowhere, everything changed: "it simply becomes a reality of my life before my foot hits the ground." Stephen was shaken at first by this experience, struggling to process what had occurred. "I straightened up and I remember some kind of a noise came out of me." After seeking guidance from friends, and confirmation that he had, in fact, not lost his mind, he set about making this vision a lived reality.

Time passed and Stephen found himself in the French Pyrenees, climbing toward Spain. What had started off as a spiritual epiphany became intensely physical. He experienced those initial stages as "very much a carnal, body-oriented, surrounding-oriented experience" as he navigated through places and feelings he had never previously encountered. "My body [was] being asked to walk… 15-to-20-mile treks every day, one after the other," and even for an experienced walker like Stephen this was daunting. He tried to keep things simple: "it was just a matter of putting one foot in front of the other, walking no matter what, and seeing if I could handle the daily walk." Nonetheless, uncertainty and concern crept in: "I can remember thinking, My God, what have I done?"

In his memoir, *Into the Thin: A Pilgrimage Walk Across Northern Spain*, he goes deeper into the doubts assailing him in that early moment.[37] "I begin to wonder. Has the ego laid the ultimate trap? Have I been a fool? Crossing a country on foot? Has this whole thing been nothing more than an elaborate delusion?" The foul weather in the Pyrenees reflected his deteriorating state of mind. "The self-doubt and fear of the absurdity of it all consume my thoughts as the rain and the climbing seem to drain my energy. My old friend desperation is lurking in the shadows of my consciousness." Despite being physically fit and approaching the ascent with a positive mindset, Stephen was deeply shaken mere kilometers into a lengthy journey. In the words of noted philosopher Mike Tyson, "Everybody has a plan until they get punched in the mouth."

Pilgrims on the Camino, particularly those walking the 780 kilometers from Saint-Jean-Pied-de-Port, France to Santiago de Compostela, Spain, often think of the pilgrimage as moving through three broad stages: the physical, the mental, and the spiritual. Stephen was certainly not alone among those pilgrims in being besieged by anxiety in those early, physical days, a consequence of placing one's life in the hands of one's feet. This is far more than a daily 30-minute stroll, after all! The rewards, however, are potentially more profound.

*   *   *   *   *

The benefits of walking are certainly not limited to the physical. Don't take my word for it; listen to a representative sampling of some of the great minds of the last few centuries. Rousseau: "I can only meditate when I am walking." Nietzsche: "It is only ideas gained from walking that have any worth." Kierkegaard: "Every day, I walk myself into a state of well-being and walk away from every illness. I have walked myself into my best thoughts, and I know of no thought so burdensome that one cannot walk away from it." Solnit: "Walking itself is the intentional act closest to the unwilled rhythms of the body, to breathing and the beating of the heart. It strikes a delicate balance between working and idling, being and doing. It is a bodily labor that produces nothing but thoughts, experiences, arrivals." Going back further, Saint Augustine is often credited with the pithy declaration: "solvitur ambulando," or "it is solved by walking."

Now, the research substantiates the philosophy. Shane O'Mara, Professor of Experimental Brain Research at Trinity College Dublin, describes many of the cognitive benefits of walking in his book, *In Praise of Walking: A New Scientific Explanation.*[38] Whereas prolonged sitting impairs blood flow through the brain, a simple two-minute, low-intensity walk every half-hour has the capacity to largely offset those negative effects.[39] Walking doesn't just undo the damage done by inaction; it has the potential to actually build a better brain. Brain functionality, and particularly learning and memory, is reliant upon the plasticity of synapses; brain cells need to be "remodeled" through the navigation of new experiences. That remodeling relies on the presence of supportive molecules, and one of the most significant for this purpose is brain-derived neurotrophic factor (BDNF). It turns out that BDNF is really, really valuable; it also makes for a highly resilient brain, allowing it to resist some of the damage done by trauma, infection, and aging. And here's the key: as O'Mara reveals, aerobic exercise supports the increase of BDNF levels, not to mention the production of new brain cells.

Walking also sparks creativity. In a set of studies conducted by Marily Oppezzo and Daniel Schwartz, participants completed a series of activities while either walking, sitting, or being pushed around in a wheelchair.[40] The results were unequivocal: in the three studies, "81%, 88%, and 100% of participants were more creative walking than sitting," while O'Mara adds that "idea production increased several-fold for walkers, in a reliable and sustained way, compared with those seated."

Finally, walking is a wonder-drug for the aging brain. As O'Mara explains, "you don't get old until you stop walking, and you don't stop walking because you're old." In one study, elderly adults were tasked with participating in low-impact walking groups just three times per week. Over the course of one year, the typical impact of aging on the learning and memory centers of the brain was reversed, by as much as two years. A growing body of literature reinforces this finding, highlighting that consistent walking can help to fend off cognitive decline. Kristine Yaffe and colleagues, to offer one example, tracked a group of nearly 6,000 women for six to eight years and revealed that greater physical activity (specifically walking in this case) was correlated with a lower frequency of cognitive decline.[41]

*   *   *   *   *

Stephen entered the "mental" stage of the Camino de Santiago when he passed through Burgos into the *meseta*, a high-elevation plateau that serves as the breadbasket of Spain. As he described it to me, "the *meseta* is either dreaded or embraced; you can't really be half-pregnant about the *meseta*."

Stephen's call to the Camino came following a staggering series of personal tragedies. He writes, "The deaths of a close friend and mentor as well as my wonderful father-in-law, the health crisis of a stepdaughter, the suicide death of my twenty-eight-year-old son, and lastly the decline and end of my marriage, all conspired to create an emotional crucifixion." Earlier in Stephen's life, he endured a period of addiction. Where one might anticipate that such a history would make him more vulnerable in the face of adversity, it instead proved instructive. As he explained, survival in the face of addiction demanded the development of a "radically different interior landscape" through which "a new self emerges" and "something fractured becomes whole." Grief would impose similar demands.

Much was fractured for Stephen as he set foot in a radically different exterior landscape. Throughout the first stage of his pilgrimage, Stephen frequently anticipated that the *meseta* would stir up potent memories and thoughts. The *meseta* delivered. As he told me, "I would be walking along, just observing the beauty and the space and the big-ness of it all, and all of a sudden I would just burst into these chest-heaving sobs." It wasn't a linear, coherent process; the emotional climax wasn't directly linked to recollections of individual events. On the contrary, "I had a sense that I was being purged of something. It wasn't necessarily important for me to know what, but something was working its way out."

Pilgrimage, Stephen asserts, "is about movement over ground and through experience," a process marked by the paired acts of "embracing and letting go." Before he arrived on the Camino, his life seemed to revolve around pain; every precious moment of light and peace that he enjoyed passed first through an agonizing crucible. But, as he walked westward along the Camino de Santiago, "in the absence of all the clutter" and through "the quieting of the ego," he was "shown another way to this."

*   *   *   *   *

The overwhelming majority of pilgrims to Banaras today travel there via mechanical modes. Nonetheless, some still opt to follow the traditional path. As Diana Eck describes it, the choice to walk "becomes for these pilgrims a kind of asceticism in which the journey itself is as purifying as the sacred destination."[42] The Aitareya Brahmana, a sacred collection of ancient Indian hymns, remains prescient on this front: "The feet of the wanderer are like the flower, his soul is growing and reaping the fruit; and all his sins are destroyed by his fatigues in wandering." The walk, itself, is healing and restorative.

Even if pilgrims choose to travel *to* Banaras by modern methods, they still often travel *through* it on foot. Roger Housden chose to follow the Buddha's path between Banaras and nearby Sarnath, which sits near the confluence of the Ganges and Varuna Rivers. He walked with burdens weighing heavily on his mind and on his chest as they had throughout his travels in India, most notably "the absence of my beloved."[43]

On this occasion, though, a new connection was sparked within Roger: "suddenly it struck me: I was actually choosing to carry this weight around with me, like some kind of identity—the suffering lover. It was like walking round all day with a heavy stone in my rib cage, though it had become so familiar I had come to see it as normal. In a flash, I saw how I was doing this to myself, like some martyr. In that instant, all the leaves of the trees began to glisten with light; the air felt electric, the ground full of vibration. I saw beyond any doubt that the true goddess, the one true Beloved, was everywhere, in every living particle. The weight slipped from my body." In his movement over ground, in his reflection through experience, Roger, too, was shown another way.

*   *   *   *   *

Walking, for all its accompanying blisters and foot soreness, can be healing. Nanna Natalia Karpinska Dam Jorgensen, a Norwegian scholar researching the potential of walking pilgrimages as self-therapy, describes how her second journey on the Camino de Santiago served as "a place to heal the pain; to reconnect with the past and memory of my father. I sensed that dealing with the sorrow in motion, and not statically as prior to the journey, gave more relief as the thoughts and emotions were on the move, as if processed and canalized in the act of walking."[44] Once again, the research reaffirms the intuition.

Much ink has been spilled on the relationship between physical exercise and mental health in recent decades. While I'll explore the broader challenges of depression and anxiety in "Looking Within," it's worth pausing here to examine what the literature has to say about the general benefits of walking for mental health. And, quite simply, it's complicated. An appreciable share of studies exploring this topic have identified positive effects of walking on depression. However, as James Blumenthal and Lephuong Ong discuss in their 2009 meta-analysis, those studies are littered with methodological limitations that make it difficult to extrapolate larger takeaways with any confidence.[45]

While researchers continue to tread lightly on asserting causality, new studies over the last decade have fine-tuned their approach. In his 2018 editorial in the American Journal of Psychiatry, Gregory Simon concluded that "exercise is a safe and moderately effective broad-spectrum antidepressant prescription—good for prevention and treatment across the spectrum of depression severity."[46] Simon was responding in part to innovative research carried out by Samuel B. Harvey and colleagues, in which they tracked a large sample of nearly 34,000 "healthy" adults over the course of 11 years.[47] In this case, "healthy" means that participants had previously shown "no symptoms of common mental disorder or limiting physical health conditions," as the researchers' goal was to gauge the effectiveness of physical exercise in preventing the onset of depression and anxiety. Their findings suggest that "12% of future cases of depression could have been prevented if all participants had engaged in at least 1 hour of physical activity each week."

There are ways, though, to intensify the experience of walking and amplify the psychological benefits, and one of the most promising lies in the realm of cognitive engagement. To this end, Jason Duvall conducted a study in which adults were given a pretty easy task: complete at least three 30-minute walks weekly for just two weeks.[48] Half of the sample, the "engagement group," received a list of "awareness plans," in which they were prompted to think deliberately about something specific, like focusing on their senses or making guesses or inferences around their surroundings while walking. The goal, Duvall explained, was "to influence how they engaged in and interacted with the physical environment."

That difference alone proved to be "more effective at producing positive changes in psychological well-being." In particular, participants displayed positive changes in both attentional functioning and feelings of frustration as a consequence of the added engagement. Duvall speculates that the prompts achieved these benefits by priming participants to have a more restorative experience, by becoming more focused on their surrounding environment. It's worth noting, though, that everyone involved in the study, whether part of the engagement group or not, displayed positive outcomes in terms of feelings of contentment. Another reminder: walking makes us feel good.

Indeed, a growing number of therapists recognize walking's healing potential, resulting in the recent emergence of "Walk-and-Talk Therapy" (WTT). Stephanie Revell and John McLeod surveyed practitioners of WTT; they reported that the practice is "more casual, collaborative, and facilitated a better therapeutic alliance," and that it "helped clients who were feeling stuck move forward in their journey more quickly."[49] Meanwhile, Denice Clark examined the client perspective, learning that they found WTT "more therapeutic than traditional therapy and felt walk-and-talk could be a less stigmatizing therapeutic alternative for individuals who find traditional, indoor therapy unappealing."[50]

* * * * *

Recovering from lung surgery, Edie—predictably—went for a walk. It was magical outside: "life was intense and vivid in a way I had never experienced before. My senses tingled with excitement. I breathed in every color, sound, and smell as if each were my first. I felt transcendent. I wanted to walk forever." Inside, she started learning about those mission bells, and in the process discovered both the extensive network of missions established by Father Junipero Serra across Alta and Baja California in the late 1700s, as well as the newly-developed California Mission Trail, an 800-mile pilgrimage that she had unknowingly walked a short part of for years already.

Edie went for another walk, her favorite local jaunt, a three-mile up-and-down called The Dish. Though she was still weak and sore from surgery, and thus moved slowly, "by the time I reached the top of the hill, an amazing physical transformation had occurred. For the first time since surgery, I was able to breathe deeply, and my pain went away completely."

In no time, all of the pieces came together. Edie would walk the mission trail as "a walk of thanksgiving, to celebrate living, and to thank God for his bountiful blessings and tender mercies." While the pilgrimage strained and stressed her still-recovering body, Edie pushed relentlessly through long, hot stages, passing through both seemingly endless urban landscapes and steep ascents. Even with cars whipping past as she delicately navigated narrow shoulders, Edie learned to walk purposefully, by which she meant "to experience wide-eyed wonder, the magical kind that we left behind in childhood." She "flowed with nature's more primal rhythm, one oblivious to hurry and rush," and remarked that "I became one with nature, with soul, with God, and I understood that I was a child of God," a connection that "made me feel whole."

While Edie's walk was inspired by gratitude for her impossible, miraculous recovery, she later realized that she was also "walking to forget." Despite being "oblivious to hurry and rush," she still pushed her pace, "hoping to leave myself and my fears behind." It wasn't working. But then suddenly, triggered by the site of a roadside memorial that was flecked with Job's tears, she was consumed by a cathartic wave of grief and sorrow, kindled by years of pent-up pain. It "swelled up inside me and poured out, assaulting my thin body. I heaved and shook with anguish, and tears cleansed the raw, open wounds... And then I could cry no more. I felt a sense of release, of lightness. As if something I had been carrying for six hundred miles had now been shed."

*   *   *   *   *

I previously explored the advantages of simply *being* in nature and, to this point, the discussion of walking has focused on the benefits of walking in almost *any* context. However, it turns out that *walking in nature* is the really good stuff.

At a time when many have shifted their physical activity indoors—running on treadmills, riding stationary bikes, and climbing artificial stairs—or into urban environments, we're learning that such exercise, divorced from a natural context, is a distinctly inferior experience. For example, Marcus Johansson and colleagues compared the impact of brisk walking on a city street with the equivalent practice in an urban park, focusing specifically on "affective and cognitive changes that are characteristic of psychological restoration."[51] Essentially, they wanted to find out if all walking offers similar reductions in stress and anxiety. The good news is that, across the board, their research revealed that walking in any context does indeed increase positive affect and decrease negative affect. However, the park walks offered two benefits distinct from being road-bound: feelings of a time crunch exhibited a greater decline, while feelings of revitalization increased for those walking alone.

Jo Thompson Coon and colleagues took a broader look at this question, reviewing and synthesizing the findings from eleven relevant studies, all of which compared indoor and outdoor exercise and its relative effect on wellbeing.[52] While most of those studies (nine of the eleven) showed *some* improvement in mental wellbeing, the benefits associated with walking outside were conspicuous: "measures of revitalization, self-esteem, positive engagement, and
subjective vitality were all greater following outdoor walking as were feelings of energy, pleasure, and delight, and there were decreases in feelings of frustration, worry, confusion, depression, tension, and tiredness. Participants reported greater enjoyment following the outdoor walk and

expressed a greater intent to repeat the experience."

Even if one can't exercise *in* nature, exercising while *looking at* nature is still beneficial. In a study conducted by Jules Pretty and colleagues, participants on a treadmill, engaged in a fast walk or light jog, were presented with one of five different sets of imagery, or (in the case of the control group) a blank white screen.[53] Once again, there were benefits to this exercise, regardless of the imagery; exercise alone resulted in lower blood pressure, higher self-esteem, and improved mood. However, exposure to "pleasant" scenery, whether urban or rural, produced an even greater benefit to self-esteem, while "unpleasant" scenery largely compromised the benefits to both self-esteem and mood. On the whole, the optimal conditions for the treadmill-bound involved imagery of pretty, rural scenery, which offered both the self-esteem boost and the most significant reduction in blood pressure. Beautiful nature is soothing, even if you're limited to 2-D representations.

While I've already discussed the potential therapeutic benefits of walking, there have been concerns raised by therapists about treating patients with particularly serious mental health conditions. For example, a major risk to people with major depressive disorder (MDD) is rumination, in which a problem or negative sentiment is rehashed, over and over, without resolution. Whereas healthy people demonstrate cognitive benefits from a walk, deeply depressed individuals, alone in nature for an extended time, might dwell on painful thoughts and emerge with deteriorated mood and memory.

Marc G. Berman and colleagues set out to examine this question, assembling a cohort of 20 participants, all of whom were diagnosed with MDD.[54] They were explicitly primed for rumination, receiving a prompt to "think about an unresolved negative autobiographical event," and then sent forth on a 50-minute walk. This process played out twice for each participant, with one walk taking place in an urban context and the other in nature. The nature walk proved to offer considerable potential for these participants, as they demonstrated increases in both mood and memory span afterward, relative to their experience on the urban walk. Of note, the effect sizes observed on a cohort diagnosed with MDD in this study were five times greater than what Berman had previously observed in an earlier study focused on healthy individuals.

Contrary to those concerns, walking in nature demonstrates the potential for all of us to process and move beyond negative emotions.

*   *   *   *   *

Like Edie and Roger, Stephen also carried burdens on pilgrimage. Having been shown another way in the *meseta*, a way beyond pain, he climbed into the Cantabrian mountains, and witnessed a changed world. "I see it all differently. No longer do I see pilgrims, I see pilgrimage; a movement toward something, a movement away, a movement of Grace." Walking on the Camino, past sources of tension and division faded; "Elegies of separation become expressions of compassionate oneness."

For pilgrims on the Camino de Santiago, among the many, varied things they carry is one or more stones, in service to an important ritual tradition along the route. Monte Irago, the highest point on the Camino, has been an important site for millennia. It certainly marked a Roman border, and during that time it was likely topped by a mound of stones, known as an "humilladero," possibly associated with the Roman deity Mercury. In time, that mound was topped with a cross made of iron: the Cruz de Ferro. While the origins of the tradition are unknown, at some point pilgrims started carrying stones from home to the cross as symbolic manifestations of guilt, shame, pain, and loss. They hope to relieve themselves of that burden here—an early blessing from the pilgrimage, some 230km before Santiago de Compostela itself.

While many pilgrims carry a single stone, Stephen had a pocketful—six of them in all. Beyond the two he carried for friends, "the remaining four stones belong, in every sense of the word, to me. Three represent the bookends of my lineage—my mother and father, and my son. I harvested them from the ground where they are buried." The fourth represented the countless others Stephen's life has been touched by, those he has helped and those who have helped him. As he approached the cross, he did so quite deliberately. "I know it's a symbolic idea," he told me, reflecting on the cross's mythic healing power. But nonetheless he found himself wondering: "what if it really works, what if I cast these stones on the pile tomorrow morning and it really works?" Intention matters; just maybe, he could see it into being.

The walk to the cross had been short, but memorable. He passed through the aged, decrepit village of Foncebadón, only recently recovered from a prolonged stretch as a virtual ghost town. "I can understand why writers have ascribed mystical and ominous experiences to this lonely, ruined outpost in the foothills," he wrote. "But even though the pilgrimage has shown me old things, there are places like this that bring time into focus for what it is—nothing and everything." Climbing higher, he paused often, taking in the magnificent views, immersed in the beauty while also reflecting on his first day's walk through the Pyrenees. "It is noticeable how differently my body feels during this climb. My breath and steps are easier now." Stephen had long left the physical stage of the Camino behind; so, too, was the mental stage now completed. Only the spiritual remained.

And yet, for all of that—the carefully assembled stones, a recognition of the need to let go, the explicit intention to do so, and the beautiful terrain offering succor—the cross stopped Stephen in his tracks. "There is a familiar feeling with me now. It's the same feeling we get at the cemetery when the funeral has ended and it's time to go; when all the beliefs about the truth of the Soul and the illusions of the body flee from us, and we are left to sit there abandoned utterly. I can't let them go. God help me, I just can't."

Awash with grief, Stephen relived the story behind those stones, revisiting every wound, re-walking those well-trodden interior landscapes. And finally, he said a prayer, and released the stones. "I finally did drop them," he concluded to me, "and then the Camino had its way." Something fractured, something whole.

*   *   *   *   *

Reflecting upon his pilgrimage on the Camino de Santiago, Sean Slavin offers some perceptive insights into how the process of walking in nature can open us wide and lay us bare.[55] "In walking I open myself to something within, which is also something in the world—something that speaks of infinity, the Milky Way, the dreams of a single night, the path unfolding past, out into the future. Still—in the moment. Yet each moment, each present, comes and goes from one infinity into another and is contained in that idea, infinity." Slavin links the internal and universal here; instead of diminishing our importance, the juxtaposition of our finite selves with the boundlessly infinite is an experience laden with potential. "This process reveals the importance of paying attention to the immediate, to what is present to us at any given moment. When the infinite, in all its intensity, can be apprehended then the finite nature of existence is revealed. The moment 'is' no more. The pilgrim is a walker walking, and the landscape is no longer a path but truly 'there' as something entirely for itself." Where we might otherwise be tempted to dwell in the heaviness of the past, or be consumed by anxiety about what is ahead, walking has the potential to embed our consciousness in the immediate now.

Intriguingly, Slavin calls attention to the expression, "fall into a rhythm," highlighting that falling is an act stripped of self-control, external to the body and mind. Similarly, he offers, that through walking "we give ourselves to a rhythm allowing it to control the body like an involuntary movement." Walking offers us the possibility of immersion in a state in which we relinquish control and find ourselves.

*   *   *   *   *

Walking doesn't have to be a solitary activity; on the contrary, there are ample benefits to making it a shared experience. I previously discussed the work done by Marcus Johansson and colleagues that compared the impact of walking in urban parks and on city streets. Their research also revealed a pair of notable findings about walking with others. First, while physical exhaustion increased when walking alone, no such effect occurred when walking with a friend. Second, while walking alone in a park produced feelings of revitalization, the effect was even greater when walking with a friend—even on city streets.

Walking groups have become increasingly popular outlets for exercise and socialization, particularly in the United Kingdom. Sarah Hanson and Andy Jones reviewed the available research on the health benefits of these groups, assembling a sample that included 42 studies with over 1800 combined participants.[56] The results were tremendously encouraging, revealing statistically significant positive outcomes with systolic and diastolic blood pressure, resting heart rate, body fat, body mass index, and cholesterol levels. Evidence also suggests improved mental health. One particularly noteworthy element of walking groups, which emerges from speculation by Lydia Kwak and colleagues, is that the social cohesion woven into the experience "may have supportive effects that encourage and sustain adherence and positive attitudes towards physical activity."[57] One of the most challenging aspects of a fitness regimen is sustaining the healthy habits over the long-term. The social aspect of walking groups improves the odds of this.

When we walk together, we feel rejuvenated and connected; the exercise, far from an ordeal, becomes a pleasure. It's no surprise that we keep coming back for more!

*   *   *   *   *

I'll explore the experience of walking together on pilgrimage in more detail in "Coming to the Table," but a few aspects of this phenomenon call for consideration here.

First, the mere act of walking together, in shared common cause, through nature towards a sacred destination, proves to be galvanizing. In Maharashtra, India, roughly a million pilgrims walk annually to the small town of Pandharpur. They do so voluntarily, with no expectation of a particular boon, simply to extend their devotion to the Hindu deity Vithoba, believed to have spent time in Pandharpur, and to experience the joy inherent in the act of pilgrimage itself. As John M. Stanley describes, the walk is strictly organized; pilgrims are sorted into groups, often by caste, village, or family, and assigned a very specific route to follow.[58] Daily distances vary widely, dictated as they are by lunar cycles, so some days are tremendously challenging.

Given the nature of the pilgrimage, the walk is particularly loaded with meaning. Pilgrims carry silver replicas of saints' feet, while even "the dust of the road on which the pilgrims' feet trod comes to be regarded as especially sacred." Where the rigor of other routes might wear on a walker, in the case of Pandharpur the discipline demanded to persist in the giving of this gift, the devotional act of walking towards Vithoba, magnifies the joy. Through it all, the collective presence of believers moving in unison reinforces the grandeur. One pilgrim described a particularly salient moment to Stanley: "Everything was in motion in the wind-swept atmosphere—the ends of the saris of women, the branches of the trees, the stalks of millet in a few unploughed fields, the walking crows, and the clouds overhead… I felt I was a drop in this vast stream of human beings, that instead of walking, I was being carried forward by the surrounding motion." As another pilgrim conveyed, "A [true] pilgrim's face is the face of joy," and it is made joyous, to a great degree, through a walk made together.

Second, shared movements offer peace and restoration. While some pilgrims still walk to Walsingham, an English village devoted to the Virgin Mary, most of the quarter-million visiting annually make the journey by car or bus. Unlike many sacred destinations, which feature a central locus of worship, Walsingham contains a mix of churches, shrines, and ruins, each with varying degrees of resonance and relevance to attending pilgrims. Unlike Pandharpur, where movement *to* the site matters most, Simon Coleman explains that at Walsingham it's movement "*through* the spaces of the village" that "is itself a kind of therapeutic restoration" (italics mine).[59] Instead of a singular, orthodox itinerary of worship, pilgrims are left free to choose which sites to visit and the order in which to do so. This is worth highlighting: even on a pilgrimage in which the journey is made largely through automated means, movement becomes a defining feature of the experience once at Walsingham: "Stations of the cross, processions, and even the less formal traversing of the village in the company of others take on sacramental significance."

Those ritual aspects prove to be particularly momentous. As one Roman Catholic pilgrim expressed to Coleman, participation in the procession engenders "a feeling of closeness, of unity, of doing the same thing, walking the same steps for the same reason. You are following the blessed sacrament." Emerging from this experience, pilgrims reported "a generalized 'peace' and sense of reconciliation, even with death," but for that last pilgrim, she simply offered that "you come away feeling good."

Finally, it's important to note that communal walking doesn't demand constant conversation. In Sweden, group pilgrimages often operate with silent stretches built into the daily schedule; indeed, in the reflections of some pilgrims, it's those moments of silence that transform the experience from a mere walk, making it more meaningful. And they almost universally like the silence, with 87% of respondents regarding it as a positive experience. Tatjana Schnell and Sarah Pali found in their research that silent walking is "conducive to self-exploration or more subconscious forms of re-arrangement of priorities; it gives access to other modes of being and seeing the world and, as a consequence, can result in the acquisition of "new" meaning, in clarification and a change of perspective."[60]

In her discussion of this phenomenon, Anna Davidsson Bremborg raises a perceptive question: "Why do the pilgrims want to walk in a group if it is silence they want?"[61] In her analysis, the "moment of silent walk separates special time for thoughts and reflections—a structural help. The other people in the group accept the silence—a social help. And finally the leaders provide some spiritual reflections and 'input'—a theological/existential help." However, even this neglects the virtues of the collective experience, virtues that have been amply discussed in the preceding pages. We are social creatures and we crave that connection, but we also construct the meaning of our experiences through reflection. A group walk with norms of silent deliberation accommodates both of those needs.

*   *   *   *   *

For the most part, Lee Hoinacki didn't walk with other people. However, he rarely walked alone. Leaving the village of Cizur Menor on the fifth day of his pilgrimage on the Camino de Santiago, he took his father's rosary in hand, mortified by the rustiness of his practice. "I am ashamed to admit that I cannot recall how many years it has been since I prayed the Rosary. I'm deeply embarrassed to find how much I've fallen into modern superstitions, abandoning ancient truths." Nonetheless, before long he found himself settling into something profound: "As I walked, I fell into a certain rhythmic pattern automatically, naturally, without any forethought or reflection." With no urgency, no schedule, he savored each word. "Each breath fitted one word; each word rested through one breath. So the prayer became a part of my body in a new way." He walked, he prayed, he walked, he prayed, and as he did so he discovered "a new way of walking over the earth, of learning to be in my place on earth."

Climbing over the Alto del Perdón (the Hill of Forgiveness) and then descending its rocky track, a section of the Camino often characterized by pilgrims as suffering from treacherous footing, Lee was consumed by awe: "I had never before seen—or dreamed of—a prayer fitting so well into a place, a time, a person, and all the surrounding circumstances—the congruences were wondrous, unforgettable."

Later in his pilgrimage, Lee reflected further on this novel experience of pilgrimage, and particularly on how walking was changing his relationship with both the natural world and his supernatural faith. Walking the Camino, "I walk into a new, very different world of touch," and "touching the *camino* with all my senses turns my body into a sensorium." This was a revelatory process, through which "I come to a felt experiencing of it, I reach a vital familiarity with it—which means that I know how it differs from all the other infinite places behind and in front of me." For Lee, the Camino took on a new function; it was not a road leading to Santiago de Compostela, but rather "a way to reach Christ—if one can learn how to walk on it." The pilgrimage is the path sanctified, "an initiatory exercise," and the "further one progresses in this way, the further one will walk into the mystery of faith."

*   *   *   *   *

When I set out to explore the available research on this subject, I knew that I would unpack the varied benefits of both walking and engaging with the natural world. That was the plan, and to some degree it played out as expected. But then, I started reading about awe. Michelle Shiota and colleagues describe the elusive pursuit of a viable academic definition of this phenomenon, before ultimately offering up this headache of an attempt: "an emotional response to perceptually vast stimuli that overwhelm current mental structures, yet facilitate attempts at accommodation."[62] Perhaps it's best to simply note that you know awe when you feel it. Helpfully, Shiota adds that most people associate feelings of awe with a natural setting.

Awe can occur in big, spectacular moments, like when you summit a mountain and are rewarded with a 360-degree view, but it can also emerge from surprisingly subtle origins. A Swedish pilgrim in Davidsson Bremborg's study described a moment in which "a sunbeam from a small [church] window fell exactly on me," and even without having lived that specific experience, the potency of that description resonates with me. In Alain de Botton's words, there "are places that, by virtue of their remoteness, vastness, climate, chaotic energy, haunting melancholy, or sheer difference from our homelands, exert a capacity to salve the wounded parts of us. These sites, valuable rather than holy, help us to recover perspective, reorder our ambitions, quell our paranoias and remind us of the interest and obliging unexpectedness of life."[63]

I'll explore the full state of the emerging research into awe in "Looking Within." For now, though, it's important to highlight that relationship between awe and nature, as this seems to offer fresh insights into why time spent in natural settings is such a positive influence in our lives. Specifically, Craig Anderson and colleagues have made two significant findings.[64] First, they established the healing potential of awe experienced through novel encounters with nature. In these direct interventions, military veterans and at-risk youth emerged from an immersive experience with distinct improvements in wellbeing and decreases in stress, when measured a week after the event. Then, they tested potentially more mundane encounters with nature—the often-brief exposure we get on a daily basis, simply going through life. Participants were asked to reflect daily on an experience of awe, or any other positive emotion, that they had felt. The researchers discovered first that participants reported higher life-satisfaction on days they encountered nature; furthermore, experiences in nature proved to be linked far more closely to feelings of awe than all other positive emotions. And, it turns out, awe is more closely linked to life satisfaction than any of those other emotions.

Nature is awesome. We should spend more time in it.

*   *   *   *   *

As we've seen, and with apologies to de Botton, the awe experienced in nature is often characterized in sacred or divine terms. This makes sense; given the limits of language, we struggle to characterize the transcendent and profound.

When nature and the sacred intersect, these are often characterized as "thin places." As Eric Weiner explains, the term likely originated in Celtic circles, "to describe mesmerizing places like the wind-swept isle of Iona (now part of Scotland) or the rocky peaks of Croagh Patrick. Heaven and earth, the Celtic saying goes, are only three feet apart, but in thin places that distance is even shorter."[65] In a more contemporary context, he continues, thin places exist "where the distance between heaven and earth collapses and we're able to catch glimpses of the divine, or the transcendent or, as I like to think of it, the Infinite Whatever."

Ann Armbrecht has spent much of her life in pursuit of thinness. She recounts her research journeys to northeastern Nepal—and her experience transitioning back into life in the USA in between—in *Thin Places: A Pilgrimage Home*.[66] Those travels, among many others, were driven by a longing "to touch some sacred essence I did not have words for." In time, Ann "experienced the sense of connection I was seeking in those moments when the veil between worlds lifted, in those thin places where I could feel the presence of the divine." Another seeker of thinness, Stephen Drew, characterized these as "revelatory places... places of unity of world and mind and spirit and body where we can see across from an illusory world into something more real." Where Ann desired the tangible, physical link, Stephen sought sight.

He's not alone. As Phil Cousineau writes, "What legendary travelers have taught us since Pausanius and Marco Polo is that the art of travel is the art of seeing what is sacred."[67] In India, we saw that the closest

Hindi match we can find for "pilgrimage" is "tirthayatra." The root of that word, "tirtha," refers to "a sacred crossing place linking this world to the Transcendent," something that sounds very much in keeping with our understanding of thin places. And Banaras is the tirtha of tirthas, the center of the earth and of creation, synthesizing all of sacred life into a *mandala*, the place where the final fording of the river of *samsara* to the shore beyond birth and death can be achieved. As Diana Eck explains, Hindus don't visit a temple or engage in pilgrimage explicitly to engage in worship; rather, they say, "I am going for *darshana*." Revealingly, darshana means "seeing."[68]

Language is a funny thing. Much like "pilgrimage," no word in Hindi is a perfect match for what we mean by "sacred." Eck indicates several words as partial fits, highlighting "pure" (*shubha, mangala*) and "good" (*punya*) as the most suitable alternatives. However, she also adds an important caveat: "we might say that in the Hindu view the whole earth is sacred, for it is all the embodiment of the Divine." The sacred, in this worldview, requires no special label as it is universal, ubiquitous. We just have to learn to see it. Pilgrimage to *tirthas*, through thin places, has the potential to show us how.

*   *   *   *   *

On one particularly memorable pilgrimage, Ann Armbrecht accompanied a small group of Yamphu men and women through the southern slopes of Mt. Everest toward Khembalung. A site of great importance to Hindus and Tibetan Buddhists alike, it is a *bhayul*, "a pure enchanted land set outside the destruction and corruption of time," thanks to the intervening magic of a Tibetan yogi. Very few actually attempt to enter the *bhayul* itself, due to the great danger involved in reaching such an inaccessible place, but instead they aim for the caves providing access to the valley, caves where gods have, for a time, resided. Even in 1992, when Ann made this pilgrimage, her presence was a rarity; Johan Reinhard had authored the first western account of a journey there only 15 years earlier.[69]

Ann's fellow pilgrims sought intercession and rewards for making the pilgrimage: "a son, a daughter, a job, a good harvest." While Ann was an experienced walker and rock climber, she seemed understandably out of her depth for much of this experience. Walking in monsoon season, ascending 11,000 feet, crossing icy streams, scaling a rock face in bare feet—feet that were numbed and bloody from the challenging conditions—Ann pushed on through it all, propelled forward by her seemingly indefatigable Yamphu companions. Finally, almost mercifully, the group passed through a waterfall and arrived in Shiva's cave, one of two caves that marked the sacred destination towards which this pilgrimage was oriented.

Johan's description of the rituals unfolding inside Shiva's cave is almost clinical in its precision. In it, we learn of the lamp lighting, offerings, prostrations, and prayer. He describes the role occasionally played by lamas, should they be in attendance. He explains the small shelf around which many rites are centered, with two tridents and two texts. Incense and chants follow.

By contrast, Ann simply declared that there "was work to be done," as the pilgrims around her launched into action. Where Johan saw worship, Ann experienced commotion, while also dwelling on her anxious anticipation of the challenging descent ahead of her. And yet, over time, she carved out the mental space to experience awe: "I imagined being here alone, with only the sounds of the wind and of the torrent of water spraying against the rock. The ground dropped steeply, and all I could see was the Barun River, silver and silent, winding its way through the green meadows far below."

Earlier in the pilgrimage, Ann recalled her first encounter with the term "thin places." It was a Quaker wedding; the groom's father described "places where one's nerve endings are bare." On this journey, she recognized, though, that the thinness wasn't solely an externalized phenomenon; rather, what "pilgrims encounter—the blessings they perceive—depends as much on their receptivity as on the sanctity of the land they pass through." Consumed by her insecurity, by the stress she felt about her capacity to keep the pace of her group, to endure the often-brutal conditions, Ann had, to some degree, closed herself off from the thinness.

And then, as her group started its return journey, she just let it all go. This opened the door: "We experience the sacred not simply by visiting places that are sacred. We enter the sacred when we let go of the fear of being exposed and begin to open our hearts to the world around us. Only when I gave up trying to hide what was inside did the boundaries between the other pilgrims and me begin to dissolve." The sacred place she sought was not physical; it had been accessible all along. She quotes Roberto Calasso here, noting that the sacred is "waiting to wake us and be seen by us, like a tree waiting to greet our newly opened eyes." The sacred is here, just waiting to be seen.

*   *   *   *   *

The sacred might even be in your own backyard. Phil Volker made his own. He didn't have a choice.

"You know," Phil told me, "there's no Stage V cancer."[70] It's the kind of joke that only someone with Stage IV cancer gets to tell. As he endured chemotherapy sessions every two weeks, Phil labored diligently to follow his doctor's prescription to use "exercise as medicine." Before long, he burned out on the hospital's small indoor gym and started hunting around for alternatives.

Around that time, Phil saw *The Way* for the first time, a film starring Martin Sheen that popularized the Camino de Santiago in the USA. It just so happens that Phil also converted to Catholicism at this moment. Four years later, Phil still marveled at the synchronicity. "Here I was... I needed something to do, I saw the movie, and I came across the idea of, well, to make it more interesting, to make it more structured, to make it more real, [why not] set up a virtual Camino? Why couldn't I just make believe that I was in Spain."

So, Phil set to work, carving out a trail in his 10 acres on Vashon Island, Washington. He had three goals: make it as long, as interesting, and as non-repetitive as he could make it. Ultimately, the finished loop covered 0.88km. When Phil started, he could only complete three laps daily; in time, he would make it 12. And five months later, after those humble beginnings, he completed his virtual journey, "arriving" in Santiago de Compostela.

Not long after, synchronicity struck again. His doctor gave him a one-cycle "vacation" from chemo, opening a window of time in which a journey to Spain could be completed. "I would go from the hospital right to the airport," Phil remembered, "and go from the airport to the hospital," but it could be done! At the same time, funds almost magically appeared to make the trip financially viable, while a small film team signed on to document the pilgrimage.[71]

Months before, Phil faced a terminal cancer diagnosis and could barely complete a 3-kilometer walk through the woods. Now, he stood on the verge of a dream come true—a dream made possible through work and faith, not to mention a small loop-trail in his backyard.

*   *   *   *   *

Lest all this discussion of the sacred sound like the exclusive realm of the religiously inclined, a series of group pilgrimages on the Isle of Man highlights the universal potential of thin places. The Praying the Keeills (PTK) initiative is a Protestant-organized week-long pilgrimage experience that includes daily walks towards Keeills, ruined medieval Celtic chapels which are the earliest known Christian sites on the island. Many of these enjoy enviable locations in places of stunning natural scenery, but none lay claim to any specific healing or divine properties.

While pilgrimage is central to the larger Christian tradition, Protestantism is largely an exception to this, making the PTK practice unusual. As Avril Maddrell speculates, that may contribute to the PTK's tendency "to focus on pilgrimage as spiritual journey," as opposed to an explicitly religious one, and the pilgrimage draws Catholics and non-affiliated walkers in addition to the majority Protestant group.[72]

Maddrell's research suggests that, for believers and non-believers participating in PTK, the primary distinctions in their reflections on pilgrimage are based more on language than experience. Both groups acknowledged benefits from being in the Isle of Man's stunning scenery, but "believers interpreted that experience in spiritual terms, as an experience of being at a numinous 'thin place' where God was especially accessible, or through making themselves open to God via the dedicated time and observances of the act of journeying on pilgrimage." That is to say, even those coming from a more secular orientation who might be less disposed to characterize nature on sacred terms still experienced similar rewards from the endeavor. Regardless of faith background, participants of all stripes found the pilgrimage to be an act of renewal, all for consistently similar reasons: physical exercise, natural setting, good company, and silence.

* * * * *

Pilgrimage offers us an opportunity to reforge a connection with the world, a connection we have lost as we've transformed ourselves into indoor, sedentary creatures. It spurs us into motion, it immerses us in natural beauty, it rekindles the senses, and it teaches us to see the numinous.

In advocating for health authorities to recognize pilgrimage as a legitimate healthcare treatment, Jorgenson succinctly identifies its potential and its limitations. "Pilgrimage walking can be regarded as a self-initiated, self-restorative self-help tool in sustaining self-health," she writes. Unfortunately, this is largely "for the privileged, since not everyone can afford such a journey [or] take a long holiday." There are, of course, pilgrimages of many different sizes and shapes, and a local, weekend experience may be more viable for most, but the caveats stand—this is an inaccessible experience for many.

However, at least *some* of the best things in life really are free! Think back to that study conducted by Anderson and colleagues on the relationship between nature, awe, and life satisfaction. Those walkers didn't need to scale mountains or journey to distant shrines. They didn't have to take a week's worth of vacation. They just went about their lives, getting the often too-brief encounters with nature that we do in our regular routines. The key, though, was to reflect explicitly on awe and other positive emotions. The more nature, the more awe; the more awe, the greater the life satisfaction. It's important to stress, though, that the awe didn't just happen; it was the prompted act of reflection that crystallized it, made it salient.

When pilgrims set out to complete the "Panchathirthi" in Banaras—a pilgrimage that links together the city's five most important tirthas—they "make a statement of intention called *sankalpa*, the explicit profession of intent to worship that accompanies every important ritual act" at every single stage.[73] When Stephen Drew reflected on thinness on the Camino de Santiago, he posited to me that "the thinness is an inside job." At a pivotal moment in his pilgrimage, when he clung to those stones—and his pain—at the Cruz de Ferro, he reflected that "the most powerful prayer I've ever said is a prayer to be willing."

We can choose to be willing.

Life will always impose its restrictions upon us, and hey, this author enjoys a good sit on a comfortable couch as much as anyone. Besides, writing this book required three solid months of being hunched over a screen. The risk we run, though, is a life spent sitting and looking, instead of one filled with moving and seeing. In the midst of the pandemic, down a lung and overloaded with preexisting conditions, Edie was still out there walking. "When things fall apart," she reflected—and with good reason, "walking helps me put the pieces back together." [74]

A better, healthier life is out there. Open your door.

LOOKING WITHIN

Pilgrimage matters at least as much for what it *isn't* as for what it is. It's not the daily routine. It's not the mundane and familiar. It's not subject to the same, habitual pushes and pulls—the incessant, unforgiving distractions—of our lives as we know them.

With more forces vying for our attention than ever before, including a seemingly infinite assortment of them conveniently stashed in our pockets, we are superficially entertained while beset with a burgeoning ennui. Only by breaking away from the known can we truly come to know ourselves and who we aspire to be. This reflective process demands time and space, two increasingly elusive qualities.

Pilgrimage provides this time and space. It allows us to see our lives from a distance, to reevaluate our priorities, and to chart a new course forward—or to simply reaffirm that we are, indeed, on the right track, so that we might appreciate it all the more.

* * * * *

"What do you want to do?"

Kym Wilson stopped dead in her tracks.[1] She had arrived at a meeting with her manager in Melbourne, Australia ready for conflict, disenchanted with her current professional arrangement and prepared to fight for something better. But when her manager placed the onus back on her, Kym's mind went blank, "like a slot machine with reels that kept spinning."

Her professional life had been unraveling for a while by this point.

She took a sabbatical in 2009 in order to pursue passion projects related to scuba diving in Asia. When she returned to work, though, she shared with me that she "really struggled being back in an office" and found that "even catching the train to work was feeling a bit claustrophobic." On the surface, it seemed like everything was in order. In her pilgrimage memoir, *The Path You Make*, Kym writes that, "I worked hard and was handed responsibility and opportunity. I built what I thought was the perfect life." And yet, she was miserable. "I cried on the way to work, on the way home and often in bed at night after my partner had fallen asleep. I isolated myself from friends in an effort to hide how imperfect my 'perfect' life was." As her professional life deteriorated, so too did her personal life, as a long-term relationship soon reached its end.

Kym was a planner. She had extensive experience with preparing and leading long-term projects. She knew that thoughtful designs often determined the difference between success and failure. However, as she faced this crisis of confidence, she despaired: "I was unable to plan my own life." After fighting this, railing against it, striving to reassert order, she found herself sinking ever deeper in quicksand. "Frustrated and scared that I didn't know what the hell I was doing, I cried. In the end, I did the only thing I could do. I gave up planning." She resigned from her job and declared it her "Year of Change."

*   *   *   *   *

You might think that, if there's one thing we can accomplish while sitting inside, it's connecting with ourselves. However, for all the time spent inside our homes, inside our workplaces, inside our cars, we struggle to find peace and clarity inside our own heads.

Early in her memoir, *Walking to the End of the World*, Beth Jusino took pains to note that she set out on her pilgrimage without any of the classic motivations.[2] She wasn't driven by a deeply spiritual purpose, she wasn't seeking insight on a pivotal question, she had no particular grief to process, and she wasn't even an outdoors person. Rather, she explains, "twenty years of postmodern adulting had burned me to a crisp. My life… was controlled by the relentless demand of screens." Beth was fortunate to love her work, to have a supportive partner, and yet, she still felt like she was missing "a life that felt real."

The one thing for sure was that Beth was *real* busy. She's not alone.

*   *   *   *   *

Sociologists have different labels for it—you'll see "time famine" and "time poverty" and "time crunch" in the literature—but they all describe the same phenomenon: a chronic, persistent busyness that defines and constrains life for many of us. In his examination of the pace of American life, John Robinson offers an entertaining overview of the proliferating published tracts on busyness: "*The Overworked American, Busy Bodies, Work Without End, Faster, The Time Divide, Fighting for Time, Work to Live, Take Back Your Time,* and *Busier Than Ever.*"[3] It's bleak out there! While this appears to be particularly salient in the USA, researchers have encountered similar concerns in other developed countries across Europe and Asia.

However, for all of that, the available literature is far more ambivalent on the accuracy of these assertions than the conventional wisdom—and the publishing world—would prime us to expect. In reviewing available survey data between 1965 and 2010, Robinson found a decrease in the percentage of Americans who self-reported being "always rushed" and having "no excess time" since the 1990s. Indeed, a higher share of Americans in 1971 and 1975 claimed to be in full-sprint mode than their peers in 2010.

Ultimately, the data right now is insufficient to measure the relative busyness of people around the world over the past century with confidence. To some degree, that doesn't matter. Rather, of greater interest than how busy we *are*, is how busy we *feel*, and what that means for our quality of life in general. In a study that tracked claims of excessive rushing across four continents, Daniel S. Hamermesh and Jungmin Lee posited their central question quite pithily: "Time Crunch or Yuppie Kvetch?"[4] After synthesizing survey data from the USA, Australia, Germany, and South Korea, they noted that higher-earning adults felt more rushed than those from other socioeconomic groupings, despite spending equivalent time working (and this includes unpaid household labor). Instead of abruptly dismissing these individuals as privileged whiners (the authors tactfully concluded that whether "one should be concerned about these complaints or simply view them as yuppie kvetching is a matter of values"), they offered an interesting takeaway. Partially as a consequence of having surplus resources, wealthier individuals feel the time restrictions more keenly, because of their greater capacity to pursue a wider array of leisure experiences. The more we *could* be doing, the more we resent being prevented from pursuing it.

Of course, the more that we think about what we *should* be doing, the less that we can enjoy any of it! Through a series of five experiments, Jordan Etkin and colleagues demonstrated that "greater goal conflict makes consumers feel more pressed for time, an effect driven by increased stress and anxiety."[5] In other words, when we have multiple conflicting uses for a free hour, we actually end up feeling worse about it—our enjoyment is diminished and even that hour feels constricted. And, oh boy, do we have conflicting uses! Beth's "postmodern adulting" included "four separate email inboxes," a calendar featuring "a rainbow of appointments, commitments, deadlines, and tasks," and persistent social media "demands" that compelled her on some days to pause between her front door and car to check Facebook. Being "off the clock" feels like an increasingly quaint notion.

This has far-reaching ramifications. Melanie Rudd and colleagues have highlighted three: those dealing with insufficient time (whether real or perceived) consume more fast food, engage in fewer leisure experiences, and volunteer less.[6] We become less healthy, less happy, and less connected.

The American president Dwight Eisenhower famously pushed aides to distinguish between "urgent" and "important" tasks, in part because he recognized that the "tyranny of the now" would inevitably push urgent-and-unimportant items ahead of more consequential matters. In his role, it was all too easy to be overwhelmed by the noise. We're all Eisenhowers today; the more we allow the urgent to overwhelm the important, the more unfulfilled we become.

*   *   *   *   *

"I had the classic midlife, existential crisis," John Brierley told me.[7] He characterized himself as "the successful businessman" with "the 2.2 children," and by social standards he had everything a man could want. One annoying problem, though: "my life was completely empty. It was devastating." John couldn't articulate what exactly had gone awry and he had no idea what was next. Just one thing was clear: "I knew I couldn't continue the way I was."

Lacking direction, John set out to reappraise his life and chart a new course. He didn't mess around, didn't try to accommodate both his old life and his new aspirations. Instead, he broke away from everything, moving into a spiritual-environmental community that is focused on personal transformation. As he explained, the community there "loves taking people who are having an existential crisis" and "re-fashioning them... so they can find themselves and go back out in the world, hopefully a little bit more useful than when they arrived."

That same year, John learned about the Camino de Santiago. Bereft of purpose, but also cleared of distraction, he would go seeking.

*   *   *   *   *

Perhaps all that time spent working would be less problematic if we loved what we were doing. Unfortunately, the story is particularly discouraging on that front.

Gallup, an American analytics and advisory company, aggregated data assembled from 155 different countries in a massive 2017 study entitled the "State of the Global Workplace."[8] On the whole, a mere 15% of employees described themselves as "highly involved in and enthusiastic about their work and workplace." By contrast, a slightly larger share of workers, 18%, are "resentful that their needs aren't being met and are acting out their unhappiness." The lion's share of employees worldwide, however, self-identify as "not engaged;" this means that 62% of working people are simply going through the motions, "putting time—but not energy or passion—into their work."

Engagement levels tend to be lower in industrial settings, where there is often less room for workers to develop and apply their own distinct strengths. This makes it particularly conspicuous that employee engagement is especially poor in Western Europe, where only 10% of workers self-identified as engaged. By contrast—and please allow me this rare moment of national pride given our poor performance elsewhere—one-third of Americans feel engaged in their jobs. Of course, while *relatively* good, this statistic is still suboptimal.

We simply cannot emerge from this disenchantment and passivity without suffering real harm. As Johann Hari explains in his book, *Lost Connections: Why You're Depressed and How to Find Hope*, a "common symptom of depression is something called "derealization"—which is where you feel like nothing you are doing is authentic or real," a sentiment that harkens back to Beth's observation.[9] It was bad enough when one had to suffer through eight hours before breaking away, but now many of us are monitoring work email from bed, checking when we first wake up and last before we finally crash. Others are at the mercy of inconsistent scheduling, facing capricious shift assignments from week to week. The work here is terrible—and such large portions!

Hari also presents notable results from a study conducted in the United Kingdom that focused on the work experiences of employees in the civil service. When other factors were equivalent—the same compensation, job status, and branch within the service—there was one key determinant in the development of depression or other forms of severe emotional distress. Those who had a higher degree of control over their work displayed far greater resilience, while colleagues with less control were more prone to adverse health consequences. Whether the work itself is inherently appealing or not, what we really need is agency, the ability to make our own distinct mark on our professional pursuits.

Most people lack this today, leaving us immensely vulnerable.

*   *   *   *   *

"Feeling like a stranger in a strange town felt better than feeling like a stranger at home." In the days after retiring from the navy, the only professional life he had ever known, Brad Genereux was adrift, burning time in Qatar as he wrestled not only with what his future might hold, but also whether he would have a future at all.[10]

Not only had he left his career, but he also bore "the extreme anxiety and trauma that was a result of [his service in] Afghanistan." As he explained it to me, "I was incredibly jumpy, anxious, and all these things were going on and I simply wasn't dealing with them… I was isolating myself more and more."[11] While Brad maintained contact with a few veteran colleagues, he otherwise suffered from a profound sense of alienation: "I felt like I had nothing in common with anybody around me."

He tried to make it work. He dutifully returned home after retirement, but, as he discusses in his pilgrimage memoir, *A Soldier to Santiago*, his "sunny plans for post-retirement didn't survive the first contact." Instead, he adds, "I discovered I was miserable back home. I felt unneeded and out of place in a boring civilian life." Leaving behind a clear purpose, he now felt useless, alone, and disconnected from everything around him. He bore not only trauma from his military service but also regrets: "[I] gave the best years of my life to a cause—to a belief that proved false."

Alienated from past and present, what was there to look forward to? "In denial about the crushing depression of having no future or even the drive to build one, I wasn't sure what work I could do anymore."

*　　*　　*　　*　　*

Depression and anxiety, along with accompanying mental health challenges, represent a growing global health crisis. A fair debate can be held on the precise magnitude of the problem, as there is some pushback on labeling it a "crisis" or "epidemic." However, the objective data alone is sufficiently alarming. The World Health Organization estimates that more than 264 million people globally suffer from depression.[12] A report authored by Kerri Smith in 2014 estimated that, around the world "it is responsible for more 'years lost' to disability than any other condition."[13]

The Commonwealth Fund found that roughly one-quarter of adults in the USA have received a mental health diagnosis or are experiencing emotional distress.[14] A.H. Weinberger and colleagues determined that depression prevalence rates in the USA "increased significantly" between 2005 and 2015.[15] While this occurred across many different demographic groupings—"the oldest age group, men, women, Non-Hispanic White persons, the lowest income group, and the highest education and income groups"—the most pronounced increase was among young people. Indeed, the deteriorating mental health of young people is a major global concern.

The USA outpaces other developed countries in clinical mental health issues. By comparison, roughly 20% of Canadians, 13% of Australians and Kiwis, and 11% of Brits have received equivalent diagnoses. However, there's an important caveat to consider here: in many countries, a stigma is associated with mental illness. Where 23% of American adults reported not wanting to see a professional about emotional distress, the same held true for 41% of British adults. Economic matters certainly come into play as well, as access to healthcare is limited in many countries. In short, we have to assume that the actual numbers of those managing mental illness is higher than the available statistics.

In *Lost Connections*, Hari's pursuit of answers to the driving forces behind this phenomenon is a very personal mission. As a teenager, he was diagnosed with depression and then prescribed gradually increasing doses of antidepressants. Early on, he felt isolated and alone with this condition. But, as time passed, he "noticed the pills appearing in more and more people's lives, prescribed, approved, recommended." Hari was no longer alone." Remarkably, he writes, when "scientists test the water supply of Western countries, they always find it is laced with antidepressants, because so many of us are taking them and excreting them." We are literally awash with antidepressants.

While the majority of us are not clinically depressed, we may still be struggling appreciably with diminished self-esteem. Many forces are influencing this—we'll get to more in a moment—but after interviewing numerous depressed people, Hari started wondering "if depression is, in part, a response to the sense of humiliation the modern world inflicts on many of us." In that case, depression sounds like a remarkably rational reaction to our all-too-short lives being consumed by unfulfilling routines.

*   *   *   *   *

When Timothy Egan embarked upon his pilgrimage to Rome, one of his goals was "to go on a digital cleanse."[16] He does not mince words: "Easy access to a world of tempting crap has clearly not been good for me. My attention span has shrunk. Sustained, deep reading and thinking are more difficult. I'm punch-drunk from the unrelenting present, the news alerts and flashes, all the chaos without context. I'm enslaved to a dopamine-induced loop, craving the brain chemical release that comes with every new text or tweet. I get lured into too much low-grade clickbait and tweets from somebody's dog."

Frankly, "tweets from somebody's dog" might qualify as upper-tier content these days.

There is a growing body of evidence that, for all the remarkable benefits provided by smartphones and social media, they are also hurting us. In a 2018 meta-analysis, Zahra Vahedi and Alyssa Saiphoo reviewed 39 different studies, including cases from North America, Europe, and Asia, that examined the relationship between smartphone usage and stress and anxiety.[17] Their analysis revealed a "small-to-medium association" across all geographic areas, though this was most pronounced in Asia.

The constant connectivity, to both email and social media, poses numerous challenges, though these manifest in different ways across age groups. Ric Steele and colleagues report that for young people, "Social media use... has been associated with a number of negative mental health outcomes, including depressive symptoms, anxiety, loneliness, suicidal ideation, and compromised quality of life."[18] However, they seem relatively untroubled by a heavier communication load. By contrast, for those over 50, like Egan, "higher numbers of sent and received mails and social media messages and more frequent checking behavior was significantly related to stress and, in turn, to burnout, depression, and anxiety."[19]

Social media demands closer consideration, as its effects are widespread and nuanced, if still evolving. Holly B. Shakya and Nicholas A. Christakis's longitudinal study of the impacts of Facebook on wellbeing offer particularly rich insights into this phenomenon.[20] They began by noting one area where the research is especially clear: face-to-face social interactions positively influence our wellbeing. That's the good news. And with that, they launched into describing the potentially negative consequences of social media usage: it pulls us away from face-to-face relationships, makes us less invested in more meaningful activities, promotes more sedentary behavior, and undermines our self-esteem. Shakya & Christakis probed that last issue more carefully and ultimately determined that increased use of Facebook (measured by the total number of "likes clicked," "links clicked," and "status updates") is, indeed, associated with negative consequences for both physical and mental health. And unfortunately, they are optimally designed to promote exactly those sorts of behavioral addictions, as Cal Newport explains in *Digital Minimalism*, leveraging our craving of social approval and positive reinforcement to monopolize our attention.[21]

It's tempting to blame the internet, smartphones, and social media for all of these problems. Plenty of articles have been published in that vein already. However, Hari asserts that modern communication technologies are neither the disease, nor even a symptom. Rather, they are a deeply flawed attempt at self-medication, a way of "escaping... anxiety, through distraction."

And thus, we conclude where we began—distraction as the alpha and omega of modern life, the impediment to us becoming who we aspire to be, and the shield that protects us from what we endure. It's a hall of mirrors and, once you're in it, it's hard to escape.

$$*\qquad*\qquad*\qquad*\qquad*$$

With apologies to Whitehead's classic line on Plato, the safest general characterization of the field of pilgrimage studies is that it consists of a series of footnotes to Victor and Edith Turner. The Turners were anthropologists who built upon Arnold van Gennep's work on rites of passage, ultimately extending it to the realm of pilgrimage. At the time, pilgrimage, despite its venerable and extensive lineage, was largely unexplored as an anthropological phenomenon. While a fair share of those footnotes link back to criticism of the Turners' theories, and certainly the field has become more nuanced over time, they essentially developed a language around which the discourse took shape.

 In van Gennep's framework, rites of passage include three stages: separation, margin (or *limen*, from the Latin for "threshold"), and reaggregation. That middle stage gives rise to one of the Turners' key contributions to pilgrimage discourse, the notion of "liminality."[22] Having embarked on pilgrimage, the ritual subject "becomes ambiguous, neither here nor there, betwixt and between all fixed points of classification." While the surrounding social structure isn't eliminated, "it is radically simplified," and the traveler experiences a place and moment "in and out of time." They later added that "liminality is not only *transition* but also *potentiality*," not only "going to be" but also "what may be." Only by breaking free of "mundane structure," by disentangling ourselves from a constraining social status, by achieving a simpler mode of being, can we create the space and time to discover and devise our potential selves.

 As a person goes through life, the Turners wrote, they gather "a store of nagging guilts." When that burden becomes unbearable, "it is time to take the road as a pilgrim." Having reviewed this extensive share of modern burdens, it's time for us to take that advice.

$$*\qquad*\qquad*\qquad*\qquad*$$

Even without mentioning it by name, pilgrims often address their pursuit of liminal space when deciding to journey forth on pilgrimage. As Phil Cousineau explains in *The Art of Pilgrimage*, we travel because of the "longing to break away from the stultifying habits of our lives at home, and to break away for however long it takes to once again truly see the world around us."[23]

 In her anthropological study of the Camino de Santiago, *Pilgrim Stories*, Nancy Louise Frey quoted a pilgrim who sought "an alternative to the dreary rhythm of daily urban life and to experience a vacation that did not entail the beach and hangovers."[24] That pilgrim later highlighted the benefits of a stripped-down social structure, replacing "the stresses of bourgeois life… with physical activity, with nature, with hardship, with solitude, with the unanticipated and novel, with less, with a new sense of time, place, and the past, and with a goal." Another pilgrim reveled in the fact that they had "no agenda, no meetings, no important people to meet and convince, no television, no papers, no reminders of the modern life."

Johnnie Walker's pilgrimage memoir, *It's About Time: A Call to the Camino de Santiago*, exemplifies this craving for liminal space.[25] Like our other John, Walker arrived at a point in his life when he simply couldn't carry on with the status quo. He writes, "I was dissatisfied with how I had become. I found that I was questioning a lot of things in my life." Now "divorced with two grown-up children," Walker doubted his "faith and the Church more and more." He "had been doing quite difficult jobs for quite a long time, for about 15 or 20 years," always "in the non-governmental sector with NGOs."[26] His last job was supposed to just last a year or two, but he stuck around for four; afterward, he "really, really wanted a change of lifestyle." Walker hadn't expected that he would accomplish this with a pilgrimage, but as he told me, "When I found out about [the Camino de Santiago], it became my bridge to a new way of life."

His memoir's title is thus both declaration and explanation. It was about damn time that he finally had a chance for this change of pace! But also, as he approached Santiago in 2006, he wondered "how I possibly could explain this experience to other people because it was quite overwhelming on a number of levels." In some ways, then, "it's about time" lays bare the experience. Pilgrimage, he explained, affords us time to dream and plan, to be intimidated by new places and people and to also embrace them, to feel exhausted and rejuvenated, to perform the daily routine while also being open to the miraculous, to hurt and to heal, and to find out what does and doesn't matter. While the external journey may be a clear, linear process, its internal equivalent is messy and circular, immersed in ambivalence and often dueling sentiments. But with time, a way emerges there as well.

There's a lovely bit of symbolism in the fact that both Johns, Brierley and Walker, found themselves on pilgrimage and then devoted their lives to helping others find their way. As Brierley told me, on his first pilgrimage he took a week of silence, pondering where he was headed. "I didn't know who I was, who I was going to become, or what I was going to be doing, but I knew that the old life that I had become used to was over." By the end of that silent week, though, "It became very clear." Despite all manner of logical objections—he didn't speak Spanish; he had never written anything for publication—Brierley would become a guidebook author. He would do so because that first pilgrimage "was huge in my life, helping me to reorientate myself, and now I was being asked to... articulate [that experience] for other people, who it might be useful for."

Walker's epiphany came a little later, when he arrived in Santiago de Compostela at the end of his first pilgrimage: "The moment that I sat in the Cathedral, I thought: this is the place for me. And so, it came to pass. I ended up resigning from the big job, I did some other things just to keep me going, and I started volunteering in the pilgrim office." Taking me back to that moment, he attempted to articulate his thinking: "If everything else in my life falls apart, if I wake up tomorrow morning and there's no money in my bank account, if I lose my house, if I lose the love of my children," he reflected, "I can survive simply with what's in my rucksack."

* * * * *

Given the overwhelming array of distractions vying for our attention, liminal space proves to be a particularly important aspect of pilgrimage today. As Francis Jauréguiberry wrote in an essay on communication technology, "Voluntary disconnection is not only a form of escape prompted by a longing for breathing space, [it's also] a need to get back to one's own pace or to have some time to oneself."[27]

In 2003 and 2004, Elizabeth Weiss Ozorak participated in a series of four rural pilgrimages in the British Isles.[28] As a professor of psychology, Ozorak was particularly interested in cognitive processes on pilgrimage. Sure, John Brierley and Johnnie Walker had transformative experiences; sure, liminal spaces sound intuitively important. But what's going on under the hood as all of this takes place?

Ozorak explained that "[t]he cognitive paradigm approaches such experiences from the perspective of information processing, asking what it is about these experiences in terms of perception, memory and meaning that renders them striking and in some way efficacious." She added that, "we do not absorb 'what's out there' like sponges" or like a video camera recording events, but rather "we draw on our own prior experiences, experiences shared by others, and rules of thumb that we have derived or been taught to create models that allow us to interpret that portion of our current environment to which we are able to pay attention." We pick and choose, fitting selected data points into pre-established cognitive structures which, in turn, transfer the information into long-term memory. Once there, a memory is likely re-packaged further, and thus "a remembered conversation will increasingly come to resemble our prototypical script." In short, we process familiar information according to familiar scripts, and over time we smooth down rough fits, making them even more familiar. Meanwhile, we respond to information that challenges those scripts with resistance. In a complex world, life's easier this way.

Having established all of that, here's the key: by separating us from the familiar, moving us into a novel context, pilgrimage "redirects and expands attention and thus influences subsequent perception and memory." In this way, the science reflects previous claims about learning to see on pilgrimage. We are more alert and engaged, and thus retain those experiences with greater precision.

In her travels, Ozorak noted many ways in which pilgrimage reduced competition for cognitive resources. First, media usage was heavily limited; despite sometimes posh accommodations, few pilgrims in the group had access to television, radio, or newspapers, and cell phone reception was rare. Second, pilgrims were not only removed from work obligations, they also were cut off from their many other life responsibilities. Mandatory chores in this new context were minimal. Meanwhile, "most pilgrims were challenged to absorb and adapt to new ways of functioning." This combination—being freed from regular cognitive demands while also being immersed in a novel context—led to cognitive processing that "seemed more thorough and less reliant on habit," which in turn "resulted in a sense of the freshness of life—of even simple things being observed more keenly than usual."

While pilgrimage offers an opportunity to liberate ourselves, temporarily at least, from our familiar scripts and schema, it doesn't actually leave us with a blank slate. On the contrary, it offers its own set of schema, though these certainly vary from place to place. On Ozorak's pilgrimages, participants operated within a Christian context, with some coordinated group activities providing space for shared religiosity. In Christianity, pilgrimage is understood to be "deeply transformative," and can catalyze the "death of the old self and birth of the new self." Given this, Ozorak concluded, "It is not surprising then that the pilgrims' new perspectives reflected that emphasis." When we set out in pursuit of transformation, and we process experiences through that lens, and we have the space to ponder the transformation we seek… well, stuff happens!

*　　*　　*　　*　　*

The Via Francigena, one of the medieval pilgrim roads to Rome, spans nearly 2000 kilometers between Canterbury, England and Rome, Italy. Before Kym set out to walk the Via in its entirety, she made a shorter foray, signing up for a week-long, pre-packaged experience along the route through Tuscany. On one hand, it was kind of a disaster. "I didn't last the week," she told me. Her feet were a mess: "I couldn't get my feet back into my shoes, they were so swollen." On the other, "it was beyond anything that I could have imagined."

Determined to now complete the full pilgrimage, Kym approached it with greater clarity. She packed and planned, and then, with mundane preparations completed, she contemplated her intentions. She determined that "they were to clarify my life purpose and to make a decision about what I wanted to do," but she also recognized that "there was a deeper meaning still unfolding that I may not fully understand until well after the physical journey had ended." Kym approached her "Year of Change" with an explicit intention of achieving personal transformation by finding her truer, deeper purpose.

But, before she could find what was next, she had to first come to terms with what had gone awry. Why, she wondered, had she always carried such a heavy burden? "Even as an adult, when I had everything to be happy about—a successful career, a loving partner, money in the bank, holidays, a great lifestyle—grief and sorrow constantly lurked in the background." Such negative emotions in the face of enviable circumstances perpetuated a deep-seated sense of shame and embarrassment: "I felt broken in some way and was ashamed of my feelings. I thought I was being ungrateful for the wonderful life I had."

Despite having made exceptional progress on the Via Francigena, crossing France and Switzerland with little trouble, Kym arrived in Italy in a tenuous position. She had looked forward to crossing from Switzerland through the historic Grand Saint Bernard Pass on foot, but bad weather forced her onto a bus. Kym broke into tears, "a weeping release as I let go of a dream." She knew she made the right choice, but she also recognized that this section of the Via Francigena "would forever be the missing middle piece of this long and winding walk." A day later, with sunny, blue skies overhead, she briefly tormented herself with "maybes," questioning her decision anew, but something different happened here: "The maybes stopped. The Pass was already past."

Leaving the town of Chatillon, she climbed sharply uphill before emerging on a plateau, the Alps towering all around her. She walked, she sang, and then she suddenly started crying. "I sobbed as I started to feel within every cell of my body that I was blessed too, not only to be here on this path witnessing all this beauty, but also to have experienced all the joy, wonder, love, grief and pain throughout my life." The pain she had carried for so many years washed back over her, but "somehow all the blame I had placed on myself started to dissolve as I sang. With it came grief for having forgotten how blessed and loved I am in the first place."

For most of her life, Kym had been fighting these feelings, striving to deny them, to reject them, and only managed to wound herself further in the process. "When I closed my heart down around my grief and pain," she writes, "I closed my heart to God." In the Alpine foothills, she started to open it back up, and in the process the ghosts of the past passed.

*   *   *   *   *

"Sacrifice," it turns out, comes from the Latin "sacrificus," which can be literally translated as "to make sacred." For many pilgrims, the suffering and hardships experienced actually make the journey more meaningful. In *Pilgrim Stories*, Frey characterizes the pain and suffering experienced by most pilgrims along the way as "the access to a rediscovery of God, a link to the past, and a strengthening of his faith in everyday miracles and God's omnipresence," and "a gift that brings greater insight." Sometimes, that kind of insight—"I'm not in pain; I'm rediscovering God!"—is better appreciated in hindsight.

While making a pilgrimage to the 88 temples on the Japanese island of Shikoku, a temple priest asked Ian Reader how his journey was going.[29] It had been a difficult day and Reader unleashed his frustrations. After listening patiently, the "priest smiled and gently reminded us that we did not *have* to do the *henro* (pilgrimage); we had chosen to do it and hence should accept the way it was. It was a *shugyō* (austerity) and hence one should not expect it to be easy, comfortable, or convenient."

Reader acknowledged the veracity of that observation, both in his own experience and that of many other pilgrims in Shikoku. He described how another pilgrim, Sato Takako, "recognizes that the value she derives from her pilgrimage is directly connected to the pains and tribulations she undergoes in it and that the tears she sheds through pain and struggle are cathartic." Something about the physical struggle opens us emotionally; it pushes us into a different mental space, where we become more receptive and vulnerable. When another pilgrim, Kagita, climbed to Temple 27, "he experienced a major turning point: as he sweated, he felt all his ills falling away." Having embarked on the pilgrimage plagued with concerning health problems, the journey was one in which "he had been expecting to die and was preparing for death." As he reached the temple, though, the journey transformed into a "pilgrimage of life."

Andreas Nordin witnessed a similar phenomenon when studying Hindu pilgrimages in the Nepalese and Tibetan Himalayas, to sacred sites including Muktinath, Pasupatinath, Kailash, and Manasarovar.[30] On the whole, 77% of the 360 pilgrims interviewed by Nordin offered a positive assessment of the hardships that they endured through the pilgrimage, while only 17% did not. Nearly two-thirds believed that their struggles "had religious value for showing respect to supernatural agents and bringing rewards, merits, blessings, wish-fulfilment, and 'fruitful' good fortune." As one pilgrim expressed to Nordin, "You can't get darshan (seeing) without hardship." Perhaps it's no surprise that nearly an equivalent number of pilgrims reported that they actively sought out hardship along the way.

Though we may not always get the hardship we want, we get the hardship we need. It serves an essential function: "Hardship was a favour according to which the right person received his or her allotted portion of life's agonies according to karmic timing, and this gave atonement for sins." This notion, of pilgrimage as penance, is certainly not unique to Hindu or Buddhist traditions; on the contrary, it was also a very common feature of medieval Catholic pilgrimage.

Many pilgrimages are not walking pilgrimages; and yet, most still impose a physical toll. Pilgrims to Mecca, for example, fly to the sacred destination and often travel by bus from sight to sight. However, they frequently describe sleep deprivation, intense heat, the crushing crowds around the Kaaba, and the frantic running in remembrance of Hagar's quest. While Reader has walked around Shikoku many times, he also participated in a bus pilgrimage as part of his research. Whereas a walking pilgrimage around the island might take seven weeks, the bus journey was a much more compact affair, with the group spending just 72 hours together and visiting only a small sample of the major shrines. What they lost in time, though, they sought to offset by a "frenetic, exhausting schedule" that involved "much haste, hard work, long hours, and very early mornings and late evenings." Ultimately, Reader acknowledged, with no little surprise, that "going by foot was less taxing." It's as though a special, concerted effort was made to preserve the visceral intensity that might otherwise be lost due to modern comforts, lest a crucial aspect of the pilgrimage experience be stripped away.

Perhaps this sounds like twisted logic. After pages spent describing the many psychological burdens we carry today, the proffered cure now is physical suffering? And agreed, at face value, that sounds ridiculous. However, the research makes a compelling case.

*   *   *   *   *

As we know at this point, walking is good for us, and walking in nature is particularly good. However, physical exertion on pilgrimage proves to be an especially rich and salient experience. In the introduction to their anthology, *Pilgrimage and Healing,* Jill Dubisch and Michael Winkelman present a helpful survey of the available literature on this subject.[31] They explain that common pilgrimage activities—not just hiking, but also "extensive dancing and other exhaustive physical activities, temperature extremes, stressful procedures, painful stimuli"—tend to "elicit the response of the endogenous opioids." This is a good thing, as it has the potential to "stimulate healing responses," while also promoting feelings of euphoria, belongingness, and certainty. Those feelings actually help to "address the psychophysiological dynamics of stress and anxiety."

The physical demands intrinsic to pilgrimage, and the often-accompanying pain and suffering, also have the potential to promote healing through their functioning as "potent mechanisms for inducing altered states of consciousness (ASC)." ASCs defy easy definitions, but Farthing's is widely accepted: "a temporary change in the overall pattern of subjective experience, such that the individual believes that his or her mental functioning is distinctly different from certain general norms for his or her normal waking state of consciousness."[32] Whether ASCs are intentionally induced, as they are in more traditional shamanic-style pilgrimages, or occur accidentally as a consequence of more generalized strain or exhaustion, Winkelman's research makes it clear that they have numerous therapeutic effects: "reduction in stress, anxiety, and psychosomatic reactions; regulation of psychophysiological processes underlying emotions, social attachments, and bonding; providing access to subconscious and unconscious information; and integration of behavioral, emotional, and cognitive processes."

*   *   *   *   *

The "Run for the Wall" is a very different kind of pilgrimage. Since 1989, American veterans of the Vietnam War have assembled in Ontario, California and traveled by motorcycle cross-country to the Vietnam Veterans Memorial in Washington DC. What started as a pair of veterans has grown into a phenomenon, with 350,000 motorcycles surging eastward to the capitol in its most recent incarnation.

Vietnam War veterans in the USA carry a particularly heavy burden, with serious war wounds compounded by traumatic homecomings that often subjected them to derision and condemnation. For decades, many have found no constructive outlet for their grief and pain, withdrawing into themselves, sequestered with "the wounds that are not visible" to the outside world.

Writing about the "Run" in 2005, Jill Dubisch first laid out the many ways in which this event qualifies as a pilgrimage: "the separation from ordinary life, the journey made under conditions of danger and hardship, the rituals performed along the way that recall the dead and the missing, the sense of liminality created by the road of a hundred or more motorcycles as they journey across the country, and the power of a sacred destination."[33] Notably, Dubisch stressed, "motorcycle riding is an intensely physical and absorbing experience... in which the pilgrim's body becomes the means and locus of both pilgrimage and healing, and may be subject to hardship and sacrifice in the process." In other words, despite the movement being provided by motorized transport, this remained a strenuous and often exhausting endeavor.

While many participants joined up "unaware that they even had any need for healing," the arc of the pilgrimage's ten-day itinerary brought many to a point of personal reconciliation. As Dubisch makes clear, though, this is not a clean, linear process; on the contrary, early healing rituals have a tendency to "first heighten the anxiety of the person being healed." Brought face to face with trauma that has been steadfastly evaded or compartmentalized for so many years places a veteran in an immensely vulnerable condition. In time, though, Dubisch finds that this increases "the power of the emotional release" later on. It's both an individual and communal process, with the larger pilgrim-veteran cohort providing succor and encouragement to those participating in the "Run" for the first time.

Dubisch concludes that this particular pilgrimage promotes healing in part by helping participants to create "a new narrative of the Vietnam War and of those who fought in it, a narrative that seeks to make meaningful the confusing and traumatic experiences that often defied such meaning." In Ozorak's framework, it's a process of authoring a new script out of old memories; in Warfield's it's a long-delayed rite of passage that offered the healing that was so critical to Brad. Arriving at the memorial, after enduring a challenging journey together, the veterans mourn and celebrate; it's easy to imagine the feelings of "euphoria, belongingness, and certainty" present in that emotional churn.

*　　　*　　　*　　　*　　　*

"Long before I understood the word 'anxiety,'" Ginny Bartolone writes, "I knew I was an anxious child."[34] She was a worrier—about everything—and having been labeled a worrier, Ginny "worried about worrying." In college, when her "debilitating anxiety came to a head," her friend helped introduce her to therapy. While this helped, after graduating, Ginny "was coming apart at the seams." That's when the same friend encouraged her to consider another type of therapy: a pilgrimage on the Camino de Santiago.

As Ginny explained it to me, "when I went on the Camino, something shifted for me as far as the way that I saw myself, the way that I saw that I treated myself, and the way that I dealt with difficult emotions."[35] She is very clear—the pilgrimage did not *cure* her anxiety or depression. Rather, as she puts it, "it broke down a lot of the tools that I was using to ignore the issues that I had."

The distractions we face aren't solely external; they can be internal, as well. Layers of rationalization and obfuscation can deflect our attention from unpleasant and inconvenient truths. The Camino stripped those away and "made everything very, very clear."

Crucially, the Camino didn't simply expose problems; it also taught Ginny to have a kinder and gentler sense of self, to recognize the importance and validity of self-care, and to feel a sense of awe over what her body could accomplish. Long embarrassed by her "bony feet," seeing them as "a burden to be fixed and hidden," she came to marvel at their power as they carried her across Spain. After years at home trying to "cover up my physical flaws," Ginny shifted her priorities to "feeling better" instead of "looking better," though she quickly learned that the former serves the latter. Instead of trying to bury or compartmentalize negative emotions, she vented to a willing audience and found the experience to be affirming and healing. And, when the daily aches and pains grew more concerning, she and her friend made the difficult choice to take a day off, swallowing their pride and giving their bodies the rest they required.

In her daily life, Ginny rarely provided herself with the care needed to be genuinely healthy. On the Camino, though, the particular set of circumstances—a vastly simplified daily routine combined with the most physically demanding challenge she had ever experienced—forced her to cultivate a more supportive and sustaining set of habits.

*   *   *   *   *

While it's easy to focus on the pain and suffering sometimes associated with pilgrimage, it's important to stress that what makes it particularly edifying and rewarding is that it's a challenge that can be met, a test we can endure. It is *just hard enough*. Mihaly Csikszentmihalyi, an acclaimed psychology professor, famously introduced the concept of "flow," which he defined as "the state in which people are so involved in an activity that nothing else seems to matter; the experience itself is so enjoyable that people will do it even at great cost."[36] And pilgrimage, for many of the reasons we've already discussed, is a flow-rich environment.

Csikszentmihalyi originally set out to answer one critical question: "When do people feel most happy?" It's a far more complicated question to answer than it might seem. To start, it's important to understand the distinction that he draws between "pleasure" and "enjoyment." Pleasure, as he defines it, "is a feeling of contentment" that we experience when our pre-established expectations, whether biologically hard-wired or socially imposed, are met. Pleasure is a good thing! However, Csikszentmihalyi asserts, that alone is not sufficient for happiness, because it does "not produce psychological growth." Contrast that with enjoyment, which one experiences when they not only meet those expectations, but also go "beyond what he or she has been programmed to do and achieved something unexpected, perhaps something even unimagined before." Enjoyment, like walking, is thus "characterized by this forward movement: by a sense of novelty, of accomplishment."

When do we feel a deep sense of enjoyment? As Csikszentmihalyi conducted research around the world—across ages, genders, and cultures—he found something quite universal. Everyone could remember "optimal" experiences, often all too fleeting, in which they felt fully in control, like "masters of our own fate," along with "a sense of exhilaration, a deep sense of enjoyment that is long cherished and that becomes a landmark in memory for what life should be like." These are conditions where everything just *flows*, and there is "order in consciousness." Crucially, Csikszentmihalyi stresses that flow states "do not occur only when the external conditions are favorable," nor are they "the passive, receptive, relaxing times." Rather, they ignite "when a person's body or mind is stretched to its limits in a voluntary effort to accomplish something difficult and worthwhile."

At the beginning of this chapter, I spotlighted John Robinson's analysis of busyness and happiness trends in America, but I held back one fascinating detail. The happiest people in the study? Those happened to be "people who were less rushed and with less excess time." More free time doesn't make us happier. Rather, having *just enough time* to accomplish something satisfying is the key. Contrast this with people sleep-walking through work. Csikszentmihalyi explains why this is harmful: without intrinsically interesting or appealing tasks, little concentration is required, and this means we are beset with "unexpected and frequent episodes of entropy interfering with the smooth run of psychic energy."

Csikszentmihalyi bluntly rejects the notion that he offers a how-to guide to happiness. These are complex, individualized processes. However, he does outline the conditions in which flow states are most likely, and those conditions align with elements often highlighted by pilgrims as distinct aspects of the experience. We achieve the first required condition when we face a task that we can complete. It must be in the realm of the possible. We also need to focus fully upon it; distractions that disrupt that focus quite understandably preclude flow. Next, the task needs to offer clear goals and immediate feedback. With those conditions met, a person then "acts with a deep but effortless involvement that removes from awareness the worries and frustrations of everyday life," exhibiting some measure of self-control as well. In the process, our sense of time is altered—it can fly by almost entirely unnoticed. Focused fully on the task, we dwell less on the self, and "yet paradoxically the sense of self emerges stronger after the flow experience is over."

Ian Reader, writing about the Shikoku pilgrimage, shares a wonderful Japanese term via the pilgrim-scholar Harada. *Henro boke* is translated as "pilgrimage immersion" or "pilgrimage senility," and it speaks to how pilgrims lose sight of the surrounding world. Harada adds that it is reminiscent of "the Buddhist notion of selflessness (*muga*)."[37]

Think back to Ginny's experience: she had a task that challenged her, but one she could complete—walking across Spain on the Camino de Santiago. Separated from the distractions at home, in a liminal space, she was able to focus on the experience itself. She received clear feedback from the trail and her body, learning how to operate in this context and engage in appropriate self-care.

Certainly, one could challenge the idea that Ginny dwelled less on the self, given how she described her process of grappling with the impact of anxiety and depression on her life while walking, but the lessons that she took from the experience highlight that transformative process described by Csikszentmihalyi. No pilgrim on the Camino de Santiago would ever claim that the entire 500-mile walk was a constant flow experience; everyone endures bad days, where the mind cannot escape the throbbing foot pain or aching knees. The tiniest blister on the tiniest toe can be a remarkably belligerent travel companion. Similarly, non-walking pilgrimages pose their own challenges, such as the complex sequences of worship that one must observe at Lough Derg, or the very precise rules that must be followed on the hajj. Nervousness over failing to adhere to these guidelines causes pilgrims to be unsettled initially, and that sometimes triggers other, deeper forms of self-doubt. Many of us have stressed about whether we are "true" pilgrims.

However, this is where the duration of many pilgrimages comes into play. A longer experience offers greater room to calm the mind and become more immersed in the act itself. In her study of the therapeutic potential of Norway's St. Olav Way pilgrimage, Jorgenson quotes one pilgrim's reflection on the experience: "It was liberating, because my brain really needed a break from stress, demands, deadlines etc. It took 5 days before it became quiet inside me. After 11 days, when I tried to think of a theme or challenge, it was as though the thoughts didn't stick to the brain anymore, but just passed by. Then, I sort of finally got a break from my thoughts."[38] There's a gradual wearing away of the tendency to perseverate on the self which, over time, creates space for flow.

Following flow experiences, whether walking through the *meseta* or completing an intensive ritual, we emerge better prepared to meet the challenges of our lives with greater confidence. In the process, Csikszentmihalyi notes, "we actually have a chance to expand the concept of who we are."

*　　*　　*　　*　　*

Kym hiked southward through Italy, leaving the snow-covered Alps behind and passing through the sprawling rice paddies of the Piedmont region. Another mountain crossing, through the Apennine range, brought her back to Tuscany, where she had first experienced the Via Francigena.

Something was changing profoundly. Having achieved some measure of personal reconciliation in the Alps, coming to terms with the guilt that plagued her from her past, her future now opened wide before her. "Every day I walked," Kym wrote, "I was becoming clearer on my purpose, especially when I wasn't thinking about it." In the moments when she "was tired and in pain or in awe of the beauty" she heard whispers of what could be, of a burgeoning desire to write and to teach. Finally, a purpose!

And yet, even as she pondered the possibility, she lacked certainty. Instead of interpreting this as a personal failure, though, or as a betrayal of her overarching pilgrimage goal, she found peace in the ambiguity. This was due, in large part, to the fact that she had recognized that her purpose and identity didn't need to be linked solely to her professional pursuits. "I wasn't scared now to walk alone into the unknown. I enjoyed my solitude and was fascinated by the mystery of what lay beyond the realms of the known. I was proud of myself, this courageous and deep woman I had become." Pilgrimage had offered her "the gift of being received for who I was," but it also bestowed upon her an expanded sense of personal capacity.

"I realized," Kym thought while overlooking the Tuscan town of Siena, "that I had walked all that friggin' way in order to learn that there is nothing I can't do. My response to this was probably predictable—You're kidding me. That's what I needed to learn?—but yes, that was what I needed to learn." The deepest truths are universally acknowledged, occasionally known, but rarely understood. A cliché made real.

*   *   *   *   *

Note that Kym pairs awe with fatigue and pain, seemingly equivalent sources of inspiration that help her find her way. After an extended discussion of the glorious struggle, it's time to return to a consideration of the downright glorious. As I mentioned in "Opening the Door," awe is remarkable stuff, increasing life satisfaction and promoting healing. It also offers great potential to help us forge a deeper connection with ourselves.

Awe helps us to escape the time crunch trap, our persistent feelings of busyness. A wonderfully insightful set of experiments conducted by Melanie Rudd and colleagues highlighted this phenomenon.[39] First, the study induced participants into feeling either awe or happiness, pairing the two emotions as they "are alike in being positively valenced and having the ability to broaden one's perspective." The results were striking. Participants who felt awe, relative to those who felt happiness, believed "they had more time available and were less impatient." Awe brought participants "into the present moment." And, "being in the present moment underlies awe's capacity to adjust time perception, influence decisions, and make life feel more satisfying than it would otherwise." Importantly, those who were induced into feeling happiness actually "perceived time as more constricted."

That's just the starting point, though. Have you ever experienced something genuinely awe-inspiring and, in the moment, felt utterly small and insignificant in the face of such grandeur? You're not alone. Whether you were in total solitude, perhaps pondering a stunning natural vista, or crushed in a sea of humanity, maybe singing along at a live music event, you were experiencing the "small-self effect" that is characteristic of awe. Indeed, in our tendency to associate awe with wild landscapes, we often neglect its capacity to bring us together and bond us more closely. As Yang Bai and colleagues described it, awe is "the quintessential collective emotion, involved in processes that lead the individual to be part of something bigger than the self, most typically social collectives."[40] Awe thus inspires greater volunteerism in two ways: by expanding our perception of time and by shifting our attention away from selfish concerns toward the greater whole. Bai critically highlighted how this phenomenon manifests across participants in both the USA and China. Whether focused on cultural contexts that favor individualism or collectivism, awe has the same effect of "integrating the individual into the collective."

Csikszentmihalyi makes it clear that there's a risk associated with this. When we orient ourselves toward pursuing pleasure, and particularly toward a notion of pleasure shaped by our surrounding culture, we run the risk of missing out on opportunities for deeper enjoyment. Extrinsic motivation is an all too appealing dead-end. However, awe offers the most positive aspects of social connection—which we require—while still empowering us to reevaluate our values and become our most authentic selves. Research conducted by Libin Jiang and colleagues indicates that awe, in particular, reduces materialism.[41] In their words, the mere act of "recalling a personal experience of awe makes people place less importance on money, compared with recalling an experience of happiness and recalling a neutral experience." Alethea Koh and colleagues added that awe also decreases negative feelings about the loss of possessions.[42] Here's why: awe empowers us to transcend more "mundane concerns" by allowing us to see our lives—and the world as a whole—in a new light. This, in turn, "enables people to reassess their goals and desires and provide new perspectives about one's purpose and meaning." As a consequence, feelings of awe often lead to a renewed consideration of religious or spiritual matters.

The magic of awe is that, in making us feel insignificant, it spurs us to rediscover significance in our lives, by reconnecting with the world around us, reevaluating what really matters to us individually, and empowering us to pursue something greater.

*   *   *   *   *

"A war waged inside of me," Brad reflected, "and I decided to wage it over the many miles I still needed to walk." Almost miraculously, in the midst of a crushing depression that had caused him to withdraw from almost everyone around him, he had discovered the Camino de Santiago and set out on pilgrimage. As he continued westward on foot through Spain, he re-lived his time in Afghanistan internally. "I'd spent years building walls inside of myself to compartmentalize the different and contradictory parts of my life. The tragedies I'd witnessed. The violence I'd been a part of. I wanted to come to terms with myself and my spotted past."

Brad described the Camino as crucible and alluded to the same three-part process that Stephen Drew experienced. By crucible, Brad explained to me, he was particularly focused on "those first two phases," from the Pyrenees through the *meseta*, "where you work the body and then you work everything on the inside. Once you grind it down and separate everything and analyze it, and then put it back together, you're a better person for it."

And yet, for all the benefits that he gained along the way, gradually opening up to both himself and the pilgrim community around him, the pivotal moment only occurred *after* Santiago de Compostela. Like many pilgrims today, Brad continued westward after Santiago, following an old Pagan tradition of walking to Finisterre—today a fishing town and tourist destination, once believed to be the westernmost point in the world. Taking me back to that moment, Brad described the extraordinary scene: "as I'm crossing that almost bare mountain ridge, that last hike before you look down on the ocean and see Finisterre in the distance, there was a massive lightning storm. There was really no cover and the choices are: do I turn back and find cover or do I just keep pushing forward." The danger was imminent and immediate: "I'm on an exposed mountain top and lightning was coming down incredibly close." However, the moment was also laden with meaning: "I felt like it was a final test… push through, whatever happens, happens… I don't know what else to do, but I'm not turning back." Awe-inducing experiences are not always safe and peaceful.

Brad emerged, not only unscathed, but also feeling like he had passed a last, crucial test. Writing in his memoir, he recalls the moment of recognition: "Dropping to my knees in the mud, I laughed. *I know who I am. I began to cry. I'm no longer lost and alone. I'm part of humanity and have been presented with a very special gift. I've been blessed with some extremely unique and personalized attention from God.*"

Having read about Brad's many brushes with death in Afghanistan,

63

circumstances that left him in a perpetual state of being "amped up, stressed and terrified," I wondered about the relationship between those moments and this one, where once again he encountered a threat to life and limb. He acknowledged that there was a connection to be made, but this time, instead of circling and perseverating, he found a way out: "there was distinctly a very real danger there, but in this case it was saying, hey, accept the fact that you're mortal and there's no fighting to be done here. This is just going through life… keep pressing forward."

*   *   *   *   *

Heather Warfield had already been exploring the potential psychological and therapeutic benefits of pilgrimage when she learned about Brad and other veterans who were fumbling their way through a transition back to "normal" life. As she explained it to me, "There are not rites of passage right now, at least in the United States, for people to have the time and space to transition away from being a military member to being a civilian."[43] While boot camp and officer development school provide a rite *into* military life, retirement is abrupt, and veterans are forced to navigate a transition that is "very difficult and often fraught with a lot of angst and questions about how one lives" largely alone.

And yet they are certainly not alone in confronting the challenge inherent to a pivotal, transitional stage in life. Where rites of passage were once a hallmark of cultures around the world, we have compressed and minimized those rites past the point of familiarity or relevance. For example, what rite of passage exists to mark one's transition into adulthood in the USA? For my high school students, it's an overnight graduation party—organized by the school and their parents. With that out of the way, it's time for a summer internship before heading off to college. Admittedly, they have a fortunate trajectory ahead of them, one likely to lead to more than sufficient material wellbeing and hopefully some measure of deeper life satisfaction. And yet, even in their case, it's a 70-year roller coaster. After an adolescent stage jam-packed with academics and extracurricular activities, to build a sufficiently appealing profile to optimize their collegiate possibilities, they are often pressed into declaring their majors within the first year of higher learning, sometimes before they even arrive on campus. Summer internships provide critical pre-professional resume-boosting opportunities, which then help them to transition swiftly to employment after finishing their undergraduate years, unless of course they're pursuing an advanced degree. Either way, eventually they're on the career track, climbing the ladder, building their brand. They have to push hard early to seize the best opportunities; they have to accelerate the pace into their prime earning years; they have to grind on later to stay relevant. Here's hoping they chose wisely about their life's purpose at the beginning of all of that!

As David Byrne sang, "And you may find yourself in a beautiful house, with a beautiful wife / And you may ask yourself, 'Well... how did I get here?'"

In *Returning from Camino*, Alexander John Shaia writes about the potential that pilgrimage offers as a rite of passage.[44] Along the way, he articulates their importance in both our past and present. First, rites challenged participants, testing them with a series of ordeals and trials, and experienced mentors helped to support participants through the process, aiding them in learning what they needed to know as they moved into their next stage of life. It was an opportunity to build capacity, to equip the self with the confidence that it is ready for what's ahead, to pass along communal wisdom. Second, and this strikes me as particularly important, Shaia highlights the communal—not individual—nature of rites of passage, explaining that "the visibility of a rite announced to the community that change was beginning, it had to be supported, and both the initiate/s as well as the community would be required to do the work of negotiating a changed relationship with each other."

Not only do we lack distinct opportunities for rites of passage, those who still choose to pursue these experiences are often met with skepticism or scorn. Think, for example, of the so-called "mid-life crisis," which might be better understood as a subconscious wail of despair, a perfectly rational response to a perception that this gift of life is slipping past. Instead of finding communal support and encouragement in the pursuit of something more meaningful, this is often regarded as an abdication of responsibility. And yet, it's clear how badly we crave and require a break from routine and distraction, an opportunity to see our lives from the outside and reflect upon their meaning and purpose.

*   *   *   *   *

Of course, while it's tempting to focus exclusively on these dramatic epiphanies and life-transforming moments, pilgrimage often has more subtle rewards, and its pilgrims more subtle needs. Sometimes, we need a nudge, not a shove—some encouragement to recalibrate and then return to "normal" life rejuvenated.

In their study on pilgrim transformations at Lourdes, a French center of Marian worship, Leighanne Higgins and Kathy Hamilton developed the concept of "mini-miracles."[45] It's important to note that Lourdes is associated most prominently with *mega*-miracles, "officially" 67 of them since 1858, when Bernadette Soubirous encountered her first apparition of the Virgin Mary. While estimates vary widely, some 3-6 million visitors are drawn to Lourdes annually, including many ill and injured, in pursuit of healing.

For all of that, Higgins and Hamilton were drawn more to less prominent events, which they characterize as "transformations that offer social, physical and peace of mind benefits to the individual." These mini-miracles were "less extraordinary" and "more frequently experienced," and still "attributed to sacred forces." Higgins and Hamilton sorted them into three broad categories. "Physical mini-miracles" involve restored health, linked in particular at Lourdes to the act of bathing in the sacred water. A priest shared a story that illustrated this phenomenon: "A lady from Paris, she had a daughter who never spoke and had tried all kinds of things, she had heard about Lourdes and came down. And she and her daughter went to the baths and prayed, etc., and on the way back in the car the daughter said 'mama...'" After they returned home, the daughter showed continued progress; in the mother's view, it was the experience at Lourdes that opened her up somehow.

"Social mini-miracles" involve a transformation that engenders a "more confident and holistic sense of self for the individual within social settings." When brothers Garry and Jacob first visited Lourdes, Garry shared that Jacob was socially disengaged, rarely joining in conversation with anyone. Every time they returned, though, he saw Jacob opening up more and more, demonstrating growing self-confidence, leading to a moment that genuinely shocked Garry. He found Jacob "standing on tables, up playing guitar and singing to all the kids." Another young Lourdes pilgrim who experienced a similar growth arc eloquently articulated this experience. She rejected the notion that Lourdes changes a person; rather, "Lourdes makes you like the person that you should be, and for a long time I had forgotten that feeling." Higgins and Hamilton concluded that these mini-miracles involved "a release of 'hidden' or 'unknown' identities resulting in a more holistic 'coherent' sense of self."

Finally, "peaceful mini-miracles" facilitate "greater peace of mind and the greater ability to cope with difficult circumstances." An elderly pilgrim noted how a conversation with a priest at Lourdes created conditions in which her "worries were able to, maybe not evaporate, but to leave me." She identified this as "a major miracle in my life."

None of those mini-miracles would pass muster with the Lourdes Medical Bureau, the official body tasked with investigating potential miracles at the shrine. However, they highlight the many different transformative forces at work on pilgrimage.

*   *   *   *   *

Where pilgrims visit Lourdes in pursuit of a miracle, pilgrims to Canindé,

Brazil have already been granted theirs. They travel to Canindé to fulfill a spiritual contract, a "promessa" (promise), that was made when they prayed for intercession by Saint Francis, a particularly popular saint in the region. Indeed, research conducted here in the 1950s found that 80% of visitors claimed to have been healed. Up to a million people travel to the shrine annually, the majority for a ten-day celebration in the fall. Most travel in the back of pickup trucks, crammed in with other passengers and bouncing along uncomfortably for long hours. Once they arrive, the central rituals involve several hours of daily church-based activities, bathing in the grotto's healing waters, and engaging in conversation with a life-size statue of Saint Francis.

This is a particularly barren part of Brazil, and its hardscrabble residents face many adverse health conditions as a consequence of poverty. In their discussion of pilgrims to Canindé, Sidney Greenfield and Antonio Mourão Cavalcante proposed a distressing theory, namely that "chronic depression and sense of helplessness may be affecting their immune systems, making them more susceptible to the ravages of illness-producing organisms."[46] The powerlessness of poverty and accompanying negative consequences of that for self-esteem only serves to exacerbate their vulnerability.

In a separate study on the Canindé pilgrimage, Lindsey King focused on the particular role of "ex-votos" in this tradition.[47] An ex-voto is a physical artifact and an offering; it is the "spiritual payment" made by pilgrims when they arrive at the shrine. Pilgrims invest great care in the creation of these, working on them sometimes for months before leaving home for Canindé. King writes that the payment of the ex-voto "reinforces a sense of self-worth in being able to fulfill a contract." Given Greenfield and Cavalcante's observations, it's easy to see why this would be especially powerful for these Brazilian pilgrims. Furthermore, King adds that "the crafting of the actual artifact may itself have the most therapeutic potential. In the crafting of an image of one's affliction, the pouring of emotion into that object, time is allowed for pondering the problem, celebrating its resolution, and the cathartic releasing of it into a tangible symbol that literally then can be cast away." The process does not sound altogether different from the stones and other objects carried by pilgrims to the Cruz de Ferro on the Camino de Santiago.

The Canindé pilgrimage takes vulnerable, powerless people and offers first hope and then agency, a possibility of healing and then the pride in holding up their end of the bargain. If the pilgrimage began with improved physical health, it concludes with a bolstered sense of self-esteem and wellbeing.

*   *   *   *   *

Contemporary life is replete with stumbling blocks in our pursuit of a healthy sense of self. Incessant distractions prevent us from focusing on what's most important, or even being able to recognize what that is. We feel incessantly busy and, as a consequence, we withdraw from activities that would make us feel better. We are depressed and anxious, or worried about friends and family members who face these challenges.

Pilgrimage offers a way out. A pilgrim on the Saint Olav Way summarizes it well: "The pilgrimage makes it possible to think a lot of yourself, your life, your future, the future of our nature and society, where you actually walk; it encourages you to trust in your own ability. You get to know what beauty and success means to you. You leave behind what disrupted your life at home. You return proud, having completed the walk and happy having met some friendly people. This, together, has a therapeutic effect."[48]

Heather Warfield adds: "pilgrimage seems to be the ultimate act of selfcare. The preparations for the journey as well as the actual pilgrimage are therapeutic. Participants in the current study reported that, once the decision was made to go on the pilgrimage, there was excitement that energized daily life. The journey also provided the context for examination of priorities, time away from responsibilities, and space to place life's experience into a framework of meaning."[49]

In practice, this plays out in varied ways for different pilgrims. Ginny and Kym found space on pilgrimage to reconcile longstanding challenges in their past, learning how to practice acts of self-kindness and care. John and Johnnie broke with careers that were no longer fulfilling and charted a new course forward. Brad rediscovered a coherent sense of self and found a future worth living, one oriented around leading other veterans on pilgrimage.

For all those distinctions, though, a bright thread runs through their collective experiences. Pilgrimage is a flow-rich environment that leads us into a liminal space, separating us from those distractions and expanding our sense of time and space. It's a challenge that can be met, an experience through which we can cultivate self-worth and peacefulness, and an opportunity to reassess what we value and who we aim to be.

COMING TO THE TABLE

Pilgrimage certainly can be a solitary affair. Kym Wilson sought out the Via Francigena specifically because it was less traveled. As she told me, "I walked 77 days by myself without seeing another pilgrim, but that was part of the attraction for me... find[ing] my own way and hav[ing] that quiet and that solitude."[1]

However, for many, the communal aspect of pilgrimage is crucial. Connecting with others in this act often creates the conditions in which the full potential for enrichment, healing, and transformation can be unleashed. Despite a proliferation of artificial "friends" on social media, in "real life" we are increasingly isolated, cut off from the social ties that can be validating, empowering, and uplifting.

Pilgrimage brings people together in an impromptu community with a shared sense of purpose. And, given all the benefits outlined in the two preceding chapters, it places us in a position to be unusually open and candid, primed to forge closer connections in this atypical context.

An African proverb sums it up well: "If you want to go fast, go alone. If you want to go far, go together."

$$* \qquad * \qquad * \qquad * \qquad *$$

For many pilgrims, adversity entails blisters, dehydration, or exhaustion. For Ann Sieben, it involved a truckload of agitated *narcotraficantes* with semi-automatic rifles trained upon her.[2]

Ann, better known as the "Winter Pilgrim," is a remarkably prolific walker. Through her first thirteen years of pilgrimage, Ann covered some 43,000 miles across 55 different countries. While she started out on well-trodden routes, like the Camino de Santiago and Via Francigena, she has since branched out, charting her own course toward sacred destinations all over the world. One year, the destination was the Santuario de Guadalupe in Mexico City; she decided to walk there from her home in Denver, Colorado. The priests she knew in Denver were not encouraging of the idea, telling her "you can't go, you're going to die, people are dangerous." Ann, however, was not easily deterred. As she told me, she confidently declared, "God protects pilgrims" and set off on her way.

Ann is also a mendicant pilgrim, in the spirit of Saint Francis of Assisi. She walks without money, trusting that people along the way will take care of her, sharing food and shelter. On journeys spanning thousands of miles, she places her life in the hands of strangers, and has never been let down. Sure, there are times when the first attempt at a night's lodging falls through, but she hasn't once been abandoned to the elements. On the contrary, she tends to have more food pushed her way than she has any hope of consuming.

And yet, for all of that, it must have been unnerving when she was alone in the heart of the Chihuahuan Desert, crossing through sand dunes away from any roads, and a vehicle suddenly came careening toward her. Ann sets the scene: "some modified pickup came by… with these big tires to drive over the rocky, sandy desert, off-road. And in the back, four assault weapons mounted in the bed of this truck, with four men with bandoliers and sidearms… They were scary looking. And then [they] pulled around to the south side of me in the direction I was going. The four men jumped out of the cab… I'm looking all around, the four men, automatic weapons right at my head…"

They besieged Ann with questions, all hurled at her with anger and insistence: "Who are you? Where are you from? What's in your backpack? Who else is with you? Where are you going?"

Operating with limited Spanish, and striving to maintain a relaxed demeanor, Ann oriented herself toward the oldest man in the group and explained, "*Jefe*, look, I am a pilgrim. I've come from Denver and I'm going to the basilica of Guadalupe." Incredulous, the man asked if she was a crazy lady, a *gringa loca*. "Look," Ann replied, "either my pilgrimage ends at Guadalupe, or my pilgrimage ends in heaven. Either way, I'm ok. You decide."

And then something remarkable happened. The *jefe* paused and then asked: "Hey, pilgrim, would you pray for me?" The dynamic shifted. Ann passed around a prayer book, so that the men could write down the names of people in their lives who they hoped Ann would pray for in Guadalupe. A moment later, the *jefe* reconsidered: "Oh, oh, well then, don't pray for me. Pray for my little boy, José. Because I don't want him growing up into this life." A younger man in the group piped up: "Would you pray for my grandma, because she's always praying for me?"

Before long, the men were struggling to find ways to support Ann in her journey, offering rides, which she rebuffed multiple times, and water, which she gladly accepted. As they parted, the *jefe* told her not to worry, that she would be "protected" on her journey.

"I don't know their lives," Ann reflected. "I can't judge everything in that man's life... He wanted me to pray for his little boy. There's a heart behind that. I can't judge him."

"I trusted that guy and it all worked out. If I didn't trust him, I probably would have been well picked apart by the birds in the Chihuahuan desert long ago... It's a great way of encountering humanity, not being afraid."

*   *   *   *   *

Sure, a willingness to place your trust in a truckload of *narcotraficantes* might be too big an ask, but the sad reality is that—particularly in the United States—we're increasingly reluctant to trust anyone. The General Social Survey has tracked trust levels in the USA since 1972, asking participants: "Generally speaking, would you say that most people can be trusted or that you can't be too careful in dealing with people?"[3] By their metrics, the USA is at historically low levels, with just 32% of Americans agreeing with that statement in 2018. (And these last few years probably aren't helping.)

Globally, trust levels vary widely across countries. The World Values Survey offers the best measurement on this front; it asks participants the following: "Generally speaking, would you say that most people can be trusted or that you need to be very careful in dealing with people?"[4] Participants are given three possible answers: "Most people can be trusted," "Don't know," and "Can't be too careful." Admittedly, there isn't much room for nuance there! Nonetheless, the results in 2014 offer a revealing snapshot of the world. The percentage of people believing that "most people can be trusted" ranges from a shockingly low 19% in Spain, through a middle tier (30-41%) encompassing the UK, USA, and Canada, up to more encouraging outcomes in China (63%) and Norway (74%). While those numbers defy easy classification, a clear trend exists: The Organization for Economic Co-operation and Development (OECD) found that trust in its member countries has declined for most of the past decade.[5]

Not coincidentally, this decline in trust has occurred in conjunction with a pattern of increasing social isolation. Robert Putnam stands at the forefront of this discourse; his seminal work, *Bowling Alone: The Collapse and Revival of American Community*, sounded the alarm way back in 2001.[6] The title captures a fascinating development that Putnam uncovered. Between

1980 and 1993, bowling grew in popularity in the USA, with the total number of bowlers increasing by 10%. However, over the same time period, league bowling dropped by 40%. It's important to pause here to note, particularly for international readers, that bowling leagues were once a common outlet for informal socialization in the USA. Bowlers joined together in four-person teams, competing against other teams each week. As such, this provided an opportunity to both spend time with close friends and to connect with an expanded social network. And suddenly, after a little more than a decade, during a period when bowling was more popular than ever, a substantial percentage of Americans were opting to do it alone, or at least in a less deliberately socialized setting.

That might sound utterly inconsequential. However, for Putnam this was symptomatic of a far more disturbing trend. Historically, Americans have led the world in participation in voluntary organizations. Even in 2000, the USA was only outpaced in this realm by a few countries in northern Europe. Nonetheless, a multi-decade withdrawal process soon became evident across all sectors. Membership in parent-teacher associations, once a bulwark of strong local education systems, plummeted. Church attendance, chronically difficult to measure, nonetheless dropped somewhere in the range of 25-50%. Labor union membership fell from 32.5 to 14.1%, while far fewer people paid membership dues for all kinds of different organizations. Americans practically stopped entertaining at home, with these events dropping 45% over two decades, and they stopped eating outside, too, with picnics declining 60%. Two-thirds of Americans expressed a preference for staying home.

These trends have not reversed in the years since Putnam published *Bowling Alone*. If anything, we have become more secluded. In his 2020 follow-up, *The Upswing*, Putnam shows that club membership and religious attendance rates have continued their stark decline.[7] Today, only roughly 20% of Americans indicate that they spend time regularly with their neighbors, while a Pew study revealed that a clear majority of Americans never meet with neighbors for parties or get-togethers. Before the coronavirus pandemic forced us to shelter in place, many of us already essentially engaged in this practice.

On the bright side, most countries in the European Union have, thus far, avoided the worst of this isolationist trend. However, research conducted by Francesco Sarracino raises concerns about trends in the United Kingdom, where 14 of the 15 favored metrics used for tracking social capital levels have declined.[8]

Isolation takes other forms, too. As Esteban Ortiz-Ospina reported in late 2019, the share of American adults "who live alone nearly doubled over the last 50 years."[9] And this *is* a global phenomenon, with single-person households becoming increasingly common around the world.

Ortiz-Ospina notes, for example, that where such solitary living circumstances were exceedingly rare in Norway and Sweden a century ago, now "they account for nearly half of all households" and are the majority in some cities. Living alone, Ortiz-Ospina stresses, is not actually correlated with loneliness, but it does align with general trends—some global, some more circumscribed—towards social disconnection.

*   *   *   *   *

Steve Watkins echoed Putnam's conclusions in his memoir *Pilgrim Strong*: "We self-seclude. I understand this in an acute way."[10] In the fall of 2012, Steve found himself in "one of the worst, most extensive depressive times of my life." As he told me, "I was one of those victims of the 2008 recession… and honestly had experienced a tremendous amount of loss in personal life, in professional life, and that dark time went on for a few years."[11]

Amid that turmoil, Steve recalled waking up one day, "completely lost and blaming myself for everything." Removed from that situation, he recognizes now that he wasn't actually at fault for all of it, "but that's what chronic depression tells you. And it tells you to give up."

At the lowest point, Steve had "taken mostly to the safety of our home, where I could keep the doors and windows closed." His most consequential daily action—when he could force himself into gear—was a trip to the mailbox. "Completely without purpose now," Steve writes, "I can't describe for you in words how much my heart hurt. I was broken."

*   *   *   *   *

"What if," Johann Hari wonders at the beginning of *Lost Connections*, "depression is, in fact, a form of grief—for our own lives not being as they should? What if it is a form of grief for the connections we have lost, yet still need?"[12]

That question has stuck with me since I first encountered it and it doesn't take much of an inferential leap to see its influence on the organization of this book. In an age of hyper-connectivity, in which we are constantly reminded of the instantaneous channels of communication linking us to all corners of the globe, earnest and authentic forms of connection prove more elusive to find. While depression and anxiety *can* be a byproduct of a neurological condition, Hari posits that they more commonly speak "to ways in which we have been cut off from something we innately need but seem to have lost along the way."

The breakdown of trust and the increase in social isolation foreshadow the phenomenon of loneliness, a subject of growing attention in recent years. Indeed, the British Prime Minister Teresa May created a new role in 2018, the Minister of Loneliness, following a report that found that nine million Brits described that they "often or always feel lonely." "Loneliness," said May, is "the sad reality of modern life."[13] While the debate rages on about whether or not this should be considered a "global epidemic"—as with depression, the data is fuzzy enough to raise questions about the growth rate—that appropriate discussion risks distracting from the heart of the matter. Whatever the ambiguity, we know that loneliness impacts many and the health consequences are potentially quite dire.

It's worth pausing here to define loneliness, as I imagine every reader sees something slightly different when presented with that word. Fay Bound Alberti built on earlier work by Anna Wierzbicka to offer the following: "Loneliness is a conscious, cognitive feeling of estrangement or social separation; an emotional lack that concerns a person's place in the world."[14] Alberti stresses that it's important to think of loneliness not as a singular emotion, but rather an "emotion cluster" that feeds on different and sometimes conflicting feelings. This is why, Alberti explains, that research has historically neglected loneliness (even if the idea of loneliness being ignored is a little *too* on the nose), as it is a construct of other more prominent emotions.

In their survey of loneliness research in 2018, John and Stephanie Cacioppo found that the "prevalence rates for loneliness in industrialized nations range from approximately 25–50% who feel lonely at least some of the time, and 5–10% who feel lonely frequently or always."[15] Based on available data at the time, they determined that loneliness was "associated with a 26% increase in the odds of premature mortality." There are particular concerns about the health consequences of loneliness for the elderly—this is an area of growing consensus in the literature—though other researchers are sounding the alarm about young adults and adolescents as well, with these trends exacerbated by the impact of social media.

In some ways, the "why" is more interesting than the "what." Hari shares the story behind John Cacioppo's early forays into loneliness studies. He started by relating a commonly understood psychobiological process: when we feel stressed, cortisol levels rise in our saliva. Cacioppo and colleagues ran study participants through an exercise in which they were asked to just go about their daily lives, business as usual.[16] At nine points over the course of a day, though, they were prompted to think about how lonely or connected they felt. Each time, they deposited a saliva sample in a tube after answering. As Hari relates, the researchers were "startled" by what they discovered: "Feeling lonely, it turned out, caused your cortisol levels to absolutely soar—as much as some of the most disturbing things that can ever happen to you."

Cacioppo explains this in evolutionary terms. Among primates, nothing is worse than being ostracized. Exclusion from the pack is, essentially, a death sentence. Cacioppo puts it slightly more delicately for humans: "A strong impulse in favor of connection simply produces better outcomes for survival." When lonely people try to sleep—and this phenomenon has manifested in studies conducted around the world—they experience a higher rate of "micro-awakenings." We all have *some* of these over the course of a night's sleep, but the fact that the lonely endure these more consistently speaks to our hard-wired perception that loneliness is perilous.

Loneliness is a vicious cycle. As Hari explains, after periods of sustained loneliness we "shut down socially" and become "more suspicious of any social contact." It spurs a state of hypervigilance, in which we become "more likely to take offense where none was intended and to be afraid of strangers." This makes loneliness a very challenging trap to escape.

What the research suggests, Hari concludes, is that you cannot break the cycle by simply finding other people. We need people "plus something else"—and specifically, we need "to feel [we] are sharing something with the other person, or the group, that is meaningful to" all involved. And, hey—I can think of something meaningful to share!

*   *   *   *   *

"You know what Camino magic really is?", Steve asked me. "Let me tell you what Camino magic really is…"

With the help and support of a loving partner, Steve emerged from his sustained period of personal darkness and discovered the Camino de Santiago. "I needed to do something," he realized, "that would make me feel strong again." A 500-mile hike was just the ticket. "There was a chance to start anew, to figure out what was ahead, and for the first time in my life I didn't really know the answers to those questions."

And yet, for all the natural splendor of the first two days of walking, he approached Pamplona in bad shape. He expected the physical adversity; a substantial percentage of pilgrims are in a similar state at the end of this opening stage. But the internal strife was more surprising. Prior to his departure, Steve had cultivated a vision of what his pilgrimage would be and planned to "approach each day quietly, reverently, carefully contemplating life's mysteries at every step." However, Steve was a journalist—by training and calling—and he swiftly felt a constant pull to connect with other pilgrims and learn their stories. He wrestled with this fear of hypocrisy, as he risked walking in a manner inconsistent with his original intention, before he finally recognized exactly what he was being called to do: *"tell the story."*

The timing couldn't have been better. Now committed to documenting others' stories along the way, Steve arrived at a pilgrim hostel in Pamplona and quickly determined that he needed to interview his host, a German man named Heinrich.

Steve told me the story: "We had this conversation about camino magic—I'm a skeptical journalist and I'm trying to get him to talk about it. And just take a moment... and think about the world that we are living in at this moment. And the circumstances that surround us and just the complete madness that we find ourselves in… But then shift your mind… think about the dynamic of what it's like to be there. For this unique moment in time, at this unique special place, there are people from every corner of the globe, who come together, and they are moving in the same direction, with the same purpose, and beyond that, we are all cheering each other on. *That* is camino magic."

*　　*　　*　　*　　*

The second major contribution of Victor and Edith Turner to the field of pilgrimage studies is the concept of "*communitas.*" The Turners assert that pilgrimage, or any liminal state more generally, largely removes social structure, allowing participants to spontaneously come together as "a homogenous, unstructured, and free community."[17] Rather utopian in vision, *communitas* "strains toward universalism and openness" and, "like man and his direct evolutionary forebears, remains open and unspecialized, a spring of pure possibility as well as the immediate realization of release from day-to-day structural necessities and obligations."

The Turners acknowledge that several distinct kinds of *communitas* exist, but in the realm of pilgrimage the first and most authentic kind—the "existential/spontaneous," which is really what's characterized above—is often superseded by the second kind, the "normative." Normative *communitas* is a pragmatic consequence that occurs when, over time, the spontaneous community becomes more established and settled. This is driven by "the need to mobilize and organize resources to keep the members of a group alive and thriving, and the necessity for social control among those members in pursuance of these and other collective goals."

There are extensive debates in contemporary pilgrimage discourse about the validity of the Turners' claims about *communitas*. Indeed, some pilgrimage experiences remain distinctly individualistic affairs. However, the phenomenon nonetheless holds true across many contemporary pilgrimages and proves to be both a defining element of transformative power and a balm for social disconnection.

*　　*　　*　　*　　*

The remainder of this book could be filled with stories of pilgrims on the Camino de Santiago echoing Steve's definition of Camino magic and singing the praises of *communitas*.

The phenomenon certainly didn't escape Nancy Louise Frey, who writes about one particularly relevant story: "One woman said she felt a strong sense of belonging and even 'home'—accepted and valued for herself—while making the Camino. Walking with a group of generally like-minded individuals, heading toward the same goal, and sharing similar pains, joys, and trials provide an opportunity for the development of friendships, love relationships, and new visions of the self as socially adept and likable."[18]

The specific logistics of the Camino de Santiago make it a *communitas*-rich environment. The substantial number of walking and biking pilgrims—especially on the most-traveled branch, the Camino Francés—ensures a broad cross-section of personalities and cultural perspectives, even in winter. The primary mode of accommodation, *albergues de peregrinos* or pilgrim hostels, offer dorm-style rooms with bunk beds. Many also feature open kitchens, where pilgrims can prepare their own meals, or shared dinners and breakfasts that bring overnighting pilgrims together. While far from lavish, and sometimes far from comfortable, these hostels have the leveling effect that the Turners ascribe to *communitas*. Frey shares the reflections from a working-class man from Burgos on this point: "He was most impressed that he was able to get to know two people who in his daily life would be out of his social reach yet who treated him as an equal. Traveling alone for the first time and for two weeks on bicycle, an electrician from La Coruña met a French professor his first day who became a close friend and a 'father figure.' They were the best two weeks of his life." Similarly, "Learning not to judge by first impression led a walker from Madrid to forge a powerful friendship with a contemporary whom he originally rejected because of a superficial dislike."

Significant socialization occurs on the trail itself, as well. Walking for perhaps 25 kilometers daily, pilgrims often fall in and out of companionship with many of their peers over the course of each stage. Chris Devereux and Elizabeth Carnegie highlight the impact of this "constant meeting and re-meeting of others on the road," noting that it "engenders a relationship in which those acts of kindness from total strangers are generously given and gratefully received."[19] That kindness, which is essentially a fundamental manifestation of Putnam's social capital, is linked to the unusual candor that permeates the walk. As one pilgrim shared with Devereux and Carnegie, "People are more open than in normal life. We had substantial conversations with all sorts." In her research, Jorgenson has posited that this "sharing of experiences, listening to and exchanging advice, has parallels in confession and psychotherapy" and results in an elevation of pilgrims' spirits and a rekindling of optimism.[20]

Those pilgrims cheering each other on, marching toward the same goal, joined in common purpose, have an intimate understanding of their collective struggles and accomplishments—they have, indeed, walked in each other's shoes. However transitory, pilgrimage forges strangers into family.

*   *   *   *   *

Similar "magic" courses through many walking pilgrimages. In her study of four separate walking pilgrimages through the British Isles, Elizabeth Weiss Ozorak observed that most pilgrims arrived with a heightened expectation of coming together as a community.[21] The mundane, daily tasks, she noted, had a galvanizing effect: "helping to carry water or wash dishes for the group and sleeping together on the floors of village halls reinforced the sense of 'being in this together.'" Ozorak characterizes this as a sense of "collective efficacy," which harkens back to the Turners' framing of "normative communitas."

Ozorak offers a particularly helpful look into one of the more complicated aspects of this community-building process. It's not always seamless. While community functioned in a positive form, making one participant report feeling "supported and affirmed by the group 'for who I really am,'" it also had a downside, as some pilgrims—more commonly women than men—worried that they might struggle to "keep up" or "that the group would somehow reject [their] 'real' self." Over time, however, many of these concerns were alleviated. Pilgrims expressed relief as they became accustomed to the routine and as the group coalesced into a community. As one woman divulged to Ozorak, "'Over the days you come together with fellow pilgrims more easily, like old friends. Whether or not you see them again, they become a part of the communion of saints.'"

On the Isle of Man, the Praying the Keeills group pilgrimage is organized around a series of daily walks, as opposed to a sustained through-hike. Avril Maddrell observed a particular "socio-spiritual" manifestation of community in this setting, with one pilgrim capturing the sentiment quite well: "I have felt close to God as we have worshipped at the keeills and walked together in this beautiful island."[22] Note the importance here of worshipping and walking *together*. This shared experience in nature links the physical world, the pilgrim community, and the divine.

The sacred shrine of the Santuario de Chimayó in New Mexico, USA draws some 300,000 pilgrims annually, with many groups converging on foot during the annual pilgrimage each Holy Week. When Paula Elizabeth Holmes-Rodman chose to participate in 1997, she was assigned to an experienced group of *guadalupana* pilgrims.[23] While her pilgrimage experience spanned just a week, it was highly strenuous, with long days of walking and a radically altered sleep schedule, as the group often rose between 2 and 3am in order to beat the heat.

From the beginning, Paula was nervous about her ability to sustain the challenging pace and endure the daily distances. The night before the first official day of pilgrimage, she badly stubbed her big toe on her motel bed, ripping off most of the toenail. The next morning, in mass, she felt "out of step" with her peers. The leader of her smaller sub-group of seven pilgrims, Maria, worked hard to reassure her. As Paula prepared for sleep, Maria came to Paula and offered her a blessing, then whispered to her, "We will love each other and travel together."

The group's walk was carefully orchestrated. They began each day with enforced silence, walking single file for the first hour. Periods of synchronized, ritualistic behavior followed, which included the singing of songs and the recitation of prayers. Opportunities for conversation were also built into the day, with pilgrims joined in pairs or groups of three, walking side by side, sometimes physically linked through held hands.

Paula struggled but pushed on. Even these difficulties, though, offered opportunities for connection. As she received first aid from a group member, that pilgrim encouraged her, telling Paula that she could "show the new girls next year" how to take care of themselves in the same way. While the community was temporary, together only for a week, it represented a long-term connection, a self-sustaining link to the future.

Similar to the Camino, shared meals also became a critical setting for communal connection. In this case, meals served to link the smaller pilgrim group with the larger community. Old women rose shockingly early to prepare breakfast, a tribal governor supplied lunch in a community center, volunteers attended swiftly to their requests—over and over, locals came together to make sure these pilgrims had the calories and care necessary to continue. However, Paula realized, "the meals are not about food," any more than "the walking [is] about exercise." Rather, "both are about sacrifice, a backing and forthing of giving and gift." This inspired Paula onward and, while she still experienced adversity, she also enjoyed periods of euphoria and contentment because of her deepening connection. "Women walked hand in hand or arm in arm, especially up the steep parts. The growing sense of communal love and common cause I feel overwhelms me."

Sacrifice and suffering proved critical for Paula. She didn't share the same core religious beliefs that motivated her fellow pilgrims, who were devout Catholics; she wasn't even Christian. Instead, "the comradeship and *communitas* I experienced emerged from the intense physicality of the venture—from the shared movement." The group's daily walking—and eating and sleeping and singing and sharing—joined them together as a unified whole, regardless of background, and imbued the experience with an even greater sense of the numinous.

*　　　*　　　*　　　*　　　*

This is not an accident. We've already seen, in "Opening the Door," that walking with others promotes feelings of restoration, improves physical health, and sustains commitment to a healthier fitness routine. It goes further, though. Paula and her Chimayó pilgrim group likely experienced what psychologists call "interpersonal synchronization." As Shane O'Mara explains, in these situations, "our breathing becomes synchronised, our heart rates must perform similar functions at similar times, and our brains simultaneously take account of what it is that the other person is likely to do, as well as monitoring and controlling what it is that you yourself are doing." Out of many walking, one group emerges.[24]

Walking together connects and liberates us. In his research on "therapeutic mobilities," Anthony Gatrell found that when we walk with other humans (or even dogs!), it "cements existing, or develops new, friendships and social interactions."[25] Meanwhile, in Scott Wiltermuth and Chip Heath's research on synchrony and cooperation, they observed that participants who walked (or sang or moved their arms) in synchronicity together demonstrated greater trust, cooperation, and self-sacrifice than people who lacked that connection.[26] While that synchronicity is sometimes intentionally engineered in group walks, classically through a marching drum, it can also develop organically.

Walking together, particularly in groups, can also prime us for spiritual experiences. Many researchers looking into the role of synchronized movement in religious communities have speculated "that synchronous movement triggers a kind of 'off switch' for self-representations in the brain," and this prepares "people for the sort of self-transcendent experience that is a hallmark of many religious practices."[27] Like awe and flow states, synchronized movement may be able to free us from dwelling on the self.

I've had countless meaningful conversations while walking with other people, conversations that stick with me to this day, but I've never felt as closely connected with someone as when walking silently in perfect synchronicity.

*　　　*　　　*　　　*　　　*

All of that said, non-walking pilgrimages certainly forge *communitas* as well. Ian Reader's intense 72-hour bus pilgrimage on the island of Shikoku is the perfect example of "temporary, transitory communities."[28]

While these pilgrims came from all over Japan, Reader characterized them as a "diverse group developing a sense of common belonging." The guide played an important part in this, organizing "collective acts of worship and prayer," both on the bus and while at temples. However, the pilgrims also arrived on the bus at a similar point in their lives, retired or semi-retired and eager to pursue something meaningful after intense careers.

Despite the trip's short duration, the experience proved to be galvanizing. Reader learned that many pilgrims, both on his bus and others, "return to the same bus company" and "come back together in the same groups year after year." The groups are coincidental in origin, but they become intentional and sustained over time as a consequence of the connections formed on pilgrimage.

In Allahabad, India, at the confluence of the Ganges and Yamuna Rivers, an annual, month-long gathering of pilgrims occurs each winter. In a typical year, the event is known as the Magh Mela and it draws millions of Hindus from all across India. Once every twelve years, though, as many as five million worshippers attend a particularly special event, the Maha Kumbh Mela.

Shruti Tewari and colleagues attended the pilgrimage in a Magh Mela year and surveyed participants both a month before and after the event.[29] They acknowledged that previous research highlighted the benefits of the "shared identity" formed in groups, and that this identity led members to both "experience mutual trust, respect and cooperation" and "expect support from their fellow group members and develop greater resilience." However, with Magh Mela, they wanted to move from studying smaller groups to a larger, collective experience. This wasn't just an increase in scale—it was a "crowded, noisy and physically-testing mass gathering"— and yet they still found "that taking part in this demanding collective event did indeed have beneficial effects."

Meanwhile, to the southwest in Pandharpur, John Stanley shared another impressive manifestation of *communitas*. A Brahmin woman (elite) and a Maratha girl (middle-peasantry), two people who were otherwise separated by social divisions in India's caste system, formed a connection on pilgrimage. Even while recognizing that the relationship would be short-lived, they found the "temporary suspension of those structures... edifying and inspiring."[30]

Perhaps most famously, the transformative impact of *communitas* profoundly influenced Malcolm X on his pilgrimage to Mecca. "During the past eleven days," he wrote, "here in the Muslim world, I have eaten from the same plate, drunk from the same glass, and slept on the same rug— while praying to the same God—with fellow Muslims, whose eyes were the bluest of blue, whose hair was the blondest of blond, and whose skin was the whitest of white. And in the words and in the deeds of the white Muslims, I felt the same sincerity that I felt among the black African Muslims of Nigeria, Sudan and Ghana."[31]

The unity forged through faith transcended race. "We were truly all the same [brothers] —because their belief in one God had removed the white from their minds, the white from their behavior, and the white from their attitude." This realization opened up new possibilities for Malcolm X. "I could see from this, that perhaps if white Americans could accept the Oneness of God, then perhaps, too, they could accept in reality the Oneness of Man—and cease to measure, and hinder, and harm others in terms of their 'differences' in color."

Once again, the communal experience, in all its varied components, joined people together. "All ate as One, and slept as One. Everything about the pilgrimage atmosphere accented the Oneness of Man under One God."

*   *   *   *   *

Rosemary Mahoney completed her year of pilgrimage in Ireland at Lough Derg.[32] She almost didn't make it. "I was tired of traveling and tired of thinking about God. It was a struggle, it was uncomfortable, and I had felt frustrated that in my holy travels belief had not suddenly dawned on me, that no great bolt of lightning had struck me. Trying to find belief was like trying to raise a heavy anchor from the bottom of the sea, an anchor whose sharp tooth had snagged beneath the iron of some sunken vessel. Stubbornly stuck at the end of a long line, it felt impossible to lift." Beyond those frustrations, Mahoney's personal life had deteriorated since her last pilgrimage: "the relationship most important to me was over, and I saw no way to retrieve it. I was bereft and wanted to get away." Nonetheless, she pushed through, drawn by an affinity for Ireland, if not for Catholicism. Besides, it's not like this pilgrimage required much of a time commitment.

Lough Derg refers to both a lake in the north of Ireland and the sacred destination situated on Station Island within it. That shrine is Saint Patrick's Purgatory. In the Middle Ages, pilgrims traveled there in pursuit of penance. After an intense two weeks of fasting and praying, those pilgrims would confess their sins and then be locked in a cave for 24 hours. If they emerged alive, they would move through another two-week cycle.

Fortunately for Rosemary, the modern pilgrimage to Saint Patrick's Purgatory is a speedier affair, spanning just three days. That said, it remains a grueling endeavor. The specific ritual guidelines, all outlined for pilgrims in a manual, are extensive and highly detailed. Adding it all up, Rosemary realized that, upon completion, she would—among other things—"have recited 891 Our Fathers, 1,404 Hail Marys, and 243 Creeds," not including any from the four masses over those three days. Maintaining the fasting tradition, she and her pilgrim peers were limited to a single meal each day, a meager affair that consisted of plain toast or oatcakes served with tea (sugar was available, but alas, no cream). The centerpiece of the experience, replacing the cave, was a 24-hour prayer vigil, stretching from 10pm on the first day through to 10pm on the second.

Recall that, in Banaras, Rosemary grappled with her inability to pray, a consequence of being "impatient and hasty, easily frustrated and reluctant to accept things as they were." Now, months later and in a difficult place emotionally, she was once more immersed in prayer, steeped in it.

Predictably, she struggled to find her way. As her cohort of 43 pilgrims moved through their first "Station," she grappled with the experience of praying in motion, but gradually found a rhythm. "The pace was odd. You prayed quickly and walked slowly… I was unused to formal prayer, unused to praying at all, but these words came easily… The repetition of the words was lulling, like the pulse of a rocking chair, and saying ten Hail Marys in a row was almost narcotic." Even then, though, she felt disconnected from her actions and those of her fellow pilgrims. "These prayers that flowed in a direction that promised consolation, guidance, and relief, but they seemed to have little to do with me."

Even in this context, with pilgrims traveling independently to Lough Derg for an intensely internal experience, wrestling with the varied personal burdens that drove them to break away from regular life for sustained prayer or penance, a community took shape. Before the vigil even began, the "shared hardship, the extremeness of it, made everyone feel close and understood." Enduring those 24 hours, though, only served to heighten that connection. "I had a sense," Rosemary reflects, "that we were putting a shoulder to an enormous wheel that we'd be heaving and turning all night. The vigil was a taste of death, but this didn't feel so bad." Note how quickly "I" became "we;" the pilgrims would endure the vigil together. However, as the night wore on, the struggle became more pronounced, despite the shared devotion: "We were beyond pushing the wheel now— the wheel had rolled heavily backward and was crushing us under it."

Rosemary couldn't go on; she went on. Exhausted and feeling "raw," she sensed the pilgrimage "stripping away my defenses." She thought about the unique dynamic between her fellow pilgrims: "We were together in a very intimate way, exposed and vulnerable, yet no one appeared to be aware of anyone else, which seemed a sign of true unity. The lack of self-consciousness grew out of an agreement: we were in it together."

Rosemary's journeys through five other sacred destinations failed to kindle her relationship with prayer. This changed in Lough Derg, though, and in this we can see the power of community and synchronized movements once more—not to mention awe's small-self effect. "We were praying in the hope that there might be some constant and responsive mercy. Thinking about the prayers in this way made it easier to see how small we truly were. And I found it wasn't so awful to acknowledge how small I was, particularly when everyone else around me was acknowledging their smallness too."

Surrounded by her fellow pilgrims, Rosemary prayed. She prayed with great focus and vigor, and "the words seemed to lift through the top of my head, my mind didn't wander." The magic of Lough Derg, as Rosemary articulates it, was being in a "place where you could be strange and extreme and obsessive on behalf of your faith—or in atonement for your sins—in the company of others similarly driven."

*   *   *   *   *

The social connection offered by pilgrimage proves to be healing in other ways, and we benefit here from a small but growing body of research conducted by scholars with expertise in psychological and medical anthropology. One of these sources of healing might be surprising, given that it involves an aspect of travel that is most commonly associated with discomfort and annoyance. As Dubisch and Winkelman explain, the experience of being in physical contact with other pilgrims, even squeezed together in crowds and buses, "engages the body at levels that are inherently therapeutic."[33]

Dubisch and Winkelman also lend insight into the value of connection for personal identity development. While we've already seen that many different factors can transform us on pilgrimage, Dubisch and Winkelman posit that on pilgrimage "the self is altered and affirmed in relationship to others," and in turn this bonding "provides mechanisms for transformation of identity."

Heather Warfield, whose education and research centers on the disciplines of psychology and counseling, brings a critical perspective to the study of the psychosocial effects of pilgrimage. Drawing upon her deep expertise, I asked her to share the best advice she could offer to pilgrims wanting to maximize their journey's healing potential. She answered, "I think being open to honest, authentic conversations with other people is a critical part of this. There are some people who want to go on a pilgrimage and then remain isolated. The people that I've interviewed indicate that this interaction piece is actually quite significant. Being able to be as you are [with] a stranger and then have that reciprocated can be quite significant in terms of healing."[34]

Wil Gesler accompanied a group of 40 Catholic pilgrims from

London on a five-day visit to the French pilgrimage site of Lourdes in 1994. Within that group, one young woman's healing experience stood out to him as particularly restorative. She was initially "nervous, distracted and reluctant to join in with the rest." To break through that isolation, "two or three of the older women in the group took her under their wings, drew her out and counseled her." She shared her story and opened up about the high-stress home environment that she had escaped by going on pilgrimage. Finally, as they returned home, "both her physical appearance and mental attitude had changed" and "she spoke cheerfully about home and family." The connection that she forged with a small group of fellow pilgrims, combined with the visit to the shrine itself, provided her with the space to process her stress and return home restored.

Gesler's personal experience on that pilgrimage is notable as well. Neither a Catholic specifically nor a religious person generally, Gesler arrived in Lourdes as a "neutral observer," admittedly one who rejected the miracle story behind the shrine. All of that said, Gesler reflects, "I can honestly say that I was psychologically and spiritually renewed. I believe that this was mainly due to the spirit of *communitas* which I felt." In his estimation, this was engendered in part by his immediate cohort of pilgrims. "For five days I was totally caught up among a group of 'good' people. They accepted me, did not wear their religion on their sleeves, answered all my questions about Lourdes and their faith honestly, and were alternately fun-loving and quietly pious, as the occasion demanded. They cared for and counseled each other." That effect was amplified by the broader community of pilgrims at Lourdes, encountered across many different settings and rituals—formally at mass, waiting together to bathe in the grotto, or marching together in the evening candle-light procession. All of this inspired a "feeling of group solidarity" and "a brief moment of epiphany" in which "the pilgrim sees the possibility of a healed world and thinks, 'If only it were always like this.'"

*　　*　　*　　*　　*

While most of the discussion thus far has centered on the power of pilgrimage to create communities out of strangers, it also offers space to strengthen and enrich existing relationships. Bob and Cindi, from Indianapolis, USA, walked the Camino Francés together after being married for 33 years. It was, Cindi told me, "the most time that we've spent continuously together ever, in our lives," and she reveled in the fact that, along the way, "every experience we had—good, bad, ugly, whatever—was shared." Bob called it "one of the best experiences I've had in my life" because of "the fact that we could walk it together," and Cindi added that "it made our relationship even stronger."[35]

Brad and Brianna, a father-daughter duo from Tennessee, USA, also walked the Camino Francés. Growing up, Brianna lived primarily with her mother, so the intensive time with her father was a marked change. "I think she found a sense of peace," Brad speculated, "just having me to herself." As Brianna shared with me, it was an opportunity to fill in gaps in her father's story: "I knew about my dad's childhood and I knew about his relationship with my mom, but… I didn't know it in… a lot of detail. Of course, on the Camino you have a lot of time to talk. I learned a ton about who he was as a younger person and about his journey as a human being." I asked Brad if there was a defining event in their trip, one that exemplified their time together, but he couldn't isolate one. "It's a bunch of moments," he recalled, "where she just lights up. Those magical moments of the two of us experiencing something we would never experience in America, not in a million years."[36]

Pilgrimage also provides an opportunity for repair and reconciliation. Growing up, Landon Roussel struggled to co-exist with his older brother Cory, who had suffered from drug addiction since early adolescence. Their relationship deteriorated, reaching its nadir when Cory threatened to kill Landon if he ever revealed Cory's habit, and the two coming to blows when Landon worried about his mother's safety. At one point, Landon moved in with a different family, just to avoid his brother. Following a stint in rehabilitation, and some tentative progress in repairing their relationship, Cory drifted, trying to find his footing, only to be imprisoned for two years.

Upon his release, Landon was there to meet him. The two had been in touch throughout Cory's incarceration, and both expressed a desire for reconciliation. Landon proposed a bold gambit: traveling to Spain and walking the Camino de Santiago. As Landon told me, "This was the experience for us to come back together."[37]

*   *   *   *   *

Cameron Powell's mother Inge had already overcome the odds. As he writes in *Ordinary Magic*, "She had beaten back cancer in 2001, aged fifty-seven, ditched the emperor of all maladies in a fiery lake of chemotherapy. Then she ran and ran and would not look back."[38] Unfortunately, nine years later, in April 2010, the emperor returned with a vengeance; Inge was diagnosed with ovarian cancer. That very same month, Cameron's marriage, which had already been on unsteady legs for years, reached its breaking point.

Inge refused to go straight back into medical treatment. "Not yet," she told the doctors, "I want to do it my way first." She recruited Cameron to join her on a pilgrimage to Santiago. He committed, of course, but that didn't change the fact that they had a complicated relationship. He carried scars from childhood, weighed down by guilt. "All my life I suffered from the hurt my irritability caused my mother." Despite years spent interrogating that irritation, he could never pin down the cause. "Was I angry at my father for abandoning us? Was I angry at my mother because as a kid I saw her angry? Did I resent the helpless-seeming part of her personality? Was I angry because my childhood had been foreshortened, even burdened, by her craving for attention, affirmation, emotional support?"

Regardless, he was angry, and his mother met that with volume. She yelled. More than that, though, "it was her anger that had scared me, far more than any fear of physical harm. Anger is the quintessential rejection: her face got red like Opa's, with veins in her forehead, and that powerful, throaty, enraged voice. Some words were in German, magnifying their terror."

Cameron grew up, settled into adulthood, and created his own life. His relationship with his mom evolved. But those childhood scars remained.

*   *   *   *   *

Landon and Cory's pilgrimage was hardly smooth. Even before they began, financial challenges forced a change in plans, resulting in a shorter walk on the Camino Primitivo—a rugged variant that follows the oldest branch of the way to Santiago. Those concerns about money added other complications, as Cory often bypassed restaurant lunches to escape the expense, meaning that the brothers spent large portions of each day apart.

Before embarking from Oviedo, they visited the cathedral, which contains some of the most revered Christian relics in Spain. As he describes in his memoir, *On the Primitive Way*, Landon sought out a priest for guidance, nervously sharing his and Cory's stories, what he hoped to accomplish on pilgrimage, and also what he feared. The priest's advice stuck with him through the days ahead: "Sometimes life presents difficulties. That's why you are on this pilgrimage. Just as you carry the burden of your backpack each day, so too will you have burdens to carry with your relationship with your brother. But remember... every day is a new stage."[39]

Landon realized that the priest was encouraging him to set aside regrets about the past, or worries about the future, and simply enjoy the time that he shared with Cory in the present. While it certainly wasn't easy, they gradually found a healthy routine, and discovered ways to chip away at some of their impediments to communication. Effective communication, of course, doesn't always require words. Landon told me about one moment that stands out in his memory: "We were walking up to the peak of Buspol and after that you eventually get to where you can see in full view the Embalse de Salime, this large hydroelectric dam. We were walking up there and it was incredibly windy, and the wind was biting our face. I think we might have even [taken] turns trying to shield each other from the wind. Just the process of us making it up that peak, there was something about it that just really bonded us together... That brotherly bonding experience we went through... there weren't a lot of words, but it drew us closer together."

The past wasn't eradicated, of course. That kind of pain doesn't just go away. "We reconciled on the Camino," Landon told me, "but it's an ongoing process to reconcile with someone you love, especially someone you have experienced hurt from." It was important and momentous, even if unfinished.

*   *   *   *   *

Like Landon, as Cameron set out on pilgrimage with his mother, he carried the burdens of a painful past, along with cynicism about what the Camino might offer him. "For the last year and a half, I would wake up in the morning feeling on my chest the entire weight of the mountains I needed to move. Like a caricature of an overachiever, I began each day unforgiven."

However, as he started walking, Cameron felt a burgeoning sense of unexpected hope. It occurred to him one day, early on the Camino, that: "It has been a very long time since I spent my time so pointlessly." He meant that in the *best* way. Freed from dwelling on his past and future, "in Spain, my mind is rarely occupied by anything more complicated than the next meal."

Immersed in the present, he also witnessed his mother's perseverance, as she pushed through all manner of physical difficulty to continue westward. He marveled at her ritual at the Cruz de Ferro, the way she "cupped her offering with both hands and held it over her head, a modest proposal to the cosmos about what she should be allowed to let go of." As they left the cross, they were both struck by how broad and smooth the trail became; Cameron suggested "that it could be indicative of our 'new beginning.'"

Cameron and Inge made it to Santiago together. Standing before the cathedral in the Praza do Obradoiro, the son marveled at the awe-inducing scene of his mother's joyful celebration: "'Look at this!' Her voice high like crying. She shakes her arms with excitement, poles waving in and out, the rivers clap their hands, the hills dance like yearling sheep. The Spanish word duende refers to a climactic show of spirit in a performance or work of art, such as at the end of a flamenco dance or bullfight. A right proper duende is what Mom now does, quivering with feeling, torn between her glances at the cathedral and the sobs each one elicits from her." It was a cathartic, transformative experience for both of them.

* * * * *

Just over a year after Landon and Cory made it home, Cory was dead. Inge passed away three years after she and Cameron returned.

Again, sometimes an epiphany is a cliché made manifest, fully and deeply understood for the eternal wisdom that, over time, was gradually distilled down into a soundbite. For Landon and Cameron, their pilgrimages with their brother and mother *had to be* about the journey that they shared together, not a destination to be reached in some unknown future. It was the time that they shared outside of time which allowed them to transcend the burdens they carried and build something new and vital.

Landon shared what the pilgrimage meant to him, especially given what unfolded afterward. "None of us are guaranteed a future with our loved ones," he writes. "If we don't cherish moments with them for what they are, we risk not cherishing our loved ones for who they are but rather who we want them to be. When I realized that all Cory wanted was for me to live with him now, the burden of our past felt much lighter."

Two years after returning from pilgrimage, Cameron's mom wrote to him on Thanksgiving, by which time treatment had failed her. In the card, she told Cameron "how grateful she was for the many months I'd put my *life on hold* to help her through *this scary journey*. But she also wanted me to be free, if I wished it. *You can go now son*, she wrote."
Cameron had one simple response, uttered aloud to an empty room: "No."

* * * * *

In most cases, the communities formed on pilgrimage are inherently temporary, a liminal space operating outside of "normal" life. For those enriched by these communities, it would be easy to see this as a bait-and-switch or a betrayal. After living through something so good, so uplifting, how can you leave it behind?

As he explains in his pilgrimage memoir, *A Million Steps*, Kurt Koontz set out on the Camino de Santiago specifically seeking "alone time for an interior journey."[40] Having retired young, this was a transitional moment in his life, a chance to chart the next stage. And yet, people kept inserting themselves in his private vigil! As one conversation led to the next, he found himself talking through deeper issues that he needed to face, and he came to recognize that "as people repeatedly come into your life, there may be a bigger reason and they should all be welcomed with open arms and a warm heart." While he still found opportunities for solitude, Kurt was drawn to the pilgrim community and its inclusive atmosphere: "On the

Camino everyone was always welcome at any table. Each person was dealing with some type of nagging physical pain, yet the conversations were always positive and uplifting."

However, Kurt was also a fast walker and he covered a lot of ground each day, thus completing longer stages than many of his peers. This meant that, as soon as he formed a new, meaningful connection, it was already at risk of breaking. As Kurt agonized over a relationship at home that was already beyond repair—he and his partner simply hadn't recognized it yet—he was compelled to cling tightly to each new person, a proxy of sorts for his heartache. Over time, though, he realized that "it was impossible for me to 'hang onto' all of the people I met along the way" and he learned to let go. "Letting go," he reflected, "creates space for the next learning experience, but equally important, allows that person to share their lessons with others."

Pilgrimage communities are temporary. They always disband. And that's okay.

*   *   *   *   *

Given the framing of this book, I recognize the risk of pilgrimage sounding like a persistently solemn endeavor, a heavy journey sometimes bordering on the dour. Indeed, life can be hard today, and the growing social disconnect is alarming. If you are lonely, or self-isolating, or feel like you lack people in your life who are trustworthy and good, I do believe you can find them on pilgrimage. Heck, you can find them within a one-mile radius of your home as well; pilgrimage just happens to prime many of its participants to be unusually open and eager for camaraderie.

Pilgrimage can also be a rollicking good time! For most pilgrims, a significant subsection of their most cherished memories involves the joyous conviviality—the great cultural fairs of the Magh Mela, shopping and negotiating together in Mecca, the uproarious nights gathered around flimsy plastic tables with Spanish wine measured in bottles, not glasses. Many go for the sacred but stick around for the secular. (Still others are surprised when the opposite occurs!)

Loneliness, we've learned, is a vicious cycle. It makes us more sensitive, hypervigilant, and wary; it causes us to alienate others and withdraw further. However, we've also learned that it is possible to break that cycle—it requires other people to connect with, plus "something else."

There are many "something elses" in this world, but I would submit that pilgrimage is a most exceptional version of it.

SOMETHING GREATER

We are meaning-hungry creatures, craving myth and mystery, answers and insights, hope and comfort. Pilgrimage provides a venue for that metaphysical and sacred pursuit, one in which the numinous seems immanent and immediate.

Admittedly, this chapter's title risks doing a disservice to its three predecessors. Certainly, we can encounter the transcendent in natural splendor; absolutely, we can be awed by our own perseverance and growth; undeniably, we can create something profound by joining together with others. All those settings are rife with potential and possibility. And yet, that hunger persists for something more.

In an age when religious affiliation is in decline, and skepticism on the rise, the pursuit of the profound persists, often following the old ways. For some, pilgrimage is obligatory, a required expression of both submission and faith. For others, pilgrimage is wholly volitional, a choice often made unknowingly, without conscious awareness of the driving force behind that decision. Regardless, it offers something greater to us all.

*   *   *   *   *

Abdellah Hammoudi was a fraud.[1] At least, he felt like one. As he embarked upon the Hajj to Mecca, he grappled with the legitimacy and appropriateness of his pilgrimage. In *A Season in Mecca*, he asserts that "I am a Muslim" who "continually questions the religion's fundaments but fiercely maintains its ethos." However, for Abdellah "the hajj had long ceased to signal salvation or a successful life." He approached the experience as much as an anthropologist as a Muslim: "I am not a believer like the others. I am approaching the hajj as I would a ritual from another religion."

Abdellah sought deeper meaning. "I was indeed," he explains, "in search of a truth of religion that could carry my life." Despite a lifetime spent connected to Islam, his views on the subject were riddled with ambivalence. "Islamic forms were the only ones that I was intimately close to and claimed as mine, that were my true home." And yet, as the years passed, Abdellah "felt more and more confined in them."

He was drawn to the hajj, pulled toward it by unknown forces. Yet he was also repelled, anxious that he would be perpetrating an offensive charade. His thoughts went to his Muslim brethren, and the fact that "faithful Muslims will, in the name of Islamic truth, be offering me a bond of solidarity and shared love; I will be receiving something precious I would have no way of reciprocating. Face-to-face with them, I will be no more than a fake." Could he, in good faith, make such a journey?

Timothy Egan described similar ambivalence in his memoir, *A Pilgrimage to Eternity.*, which documents his journey on the Via Francigena, the pilgrims' road from Canterbury to Rome.[2] Initially, he characterized his objectives in nearly archaeological terms, as he expressed a desire to "experience layers of time on consecrated ground" in service to "an attempt to find God in Europe before God is gone."

He then bluntly acknowledged a more personal goal: "I'm looking for something stronger: a stiff shot of no-bullshit spirituality." A growing impatience with his own agnosticism pushed him into action. "It's time to force the issue, to decide what I believe or admit what I don't."

Like Abdellah, Timothy grew up immersed in a faith community; he was an "Irish Catholic, by baptism, culture, and upbringing." However, that faith introduced trauma and tragedy into his life. While he acknowledged that one "sibling was made whole by religion, after losing a son to murder and finding that no one but God could salve her wounds," another was "nearly destroyed by religion." A young priest in the Egan family's parish was later exposed as one of the countless predators operating within the Catholic Church. Timothy's youngest brother and his friends fell within the priest's orbit; in time, the abuse that his brother's best friend endured led to suicide.

As Egan walked toward Rome, he dwelled on the paradox of "how a belief founded on a gospel of love could cause so much pain."

*   *   *   *   *

Year after year, the developed world is becoming less religious. The Pew Research Center found that prevalence of Christianity declined by 12% between 2009 and 2019 in the USA, with much of that gap filled by the religiously unaffiliated, which rose by 9% over the same period.[3]

Meanwhile, in Canada, an earlier Pew study tracked religious affiliation over four decades and found a marked decline among Catholics and Protestants—down 8% and 14% respectively—and an equivalent surge among the unaffiliated, 20%.[4]

In England, membership in the Anglican Church dropped from 31 to 14% between 2002 and 2018 and this headline from an Independent article rings even more ominously: "Church of England staring at oblivion as just 2% of young Britons say they identify with it."[5] This speaks to a notable trend that Pew uncovered in its research: around the world, younger people (those under 40) are less likely to be religious than their elders in 41 countries. (Only Ghana and Chad bucked the trend, with a more faithful younger crowd, but given that the median age in those countries is 21 and 17 respectively, that probably doesn't mean much.) Certainly, it makes sense that religious affiliation would increase with age, given how values and priorities shift over time, but the figures remain alarming for religious leaders.

It's also critical to note that self-identified religious affiliation hardly tells the whole story. As Egan mentions, while 53% of French people self-identify as Catholic, only 5% actually attend Mass regularly.

A 2018 Pew global study gauged religiosity across Europe with questions that cut across different faith groups.[6] Two questions in the study generated particularly relevant data. First, Pew asked respondents if they consider themselves "highly religious." In France, just 12% of the population answered in the affirmative. That figure held roughly consistent across the United Kingdom, Germany, and Switzerland, though it rebounded a bit in southern Europe, climbing to 27% in Italy and even 37% in Portugal. Those are the stalwarts, but let's open the aperture a bit. Consider the percentage of respondents in each country who indicate that they attended worship services not daily, not weekly, but at least *monthly*. For the northern countries, the affirmatives climb into the twentieth percentile range, stretching from the UK at a clean 20% up to Switzerland at 29%. Italy rises to 43%, while Portugal drops a tick, down to 36%. All of those statistics can be synthesized into a single, stunning takeaway: there is no country in Western Europe where a majority of people attend religious services even monthly!

If we take those attendance statistics at face value—and people notoriously overstate such self-reported figures—it becomes clear that connection with an organized religion does not play a central role in the lives of the majority of people in the developed world today. And further decline seems inevitable.

*　　*　　*　　*　　*

Guy Stagg didn't tell anyone the real reason that he chose to walk from Canterbury to the Holy Land. He couldn't. Emerging from a "time of unhappy confusion" triggered by a nervous breakdown, Guy was moving forward but he "was not better. Or rather I was better, yet less, much less, than I had once been. Brittle now, and hollow too, and knocked down by the slightest of blows." Facing that, he explained in his memoir, *The Crossway*, "I walked to mend myself."[7]

However, Guy felt too ashamed to admit that core motivation. He didn't believe in God, miracles, or the notion that a ritual can cure illness, and thus, in a way, his actions defied his beliefs.

Guy departed home on New Year's Day, defying the more common practice of leaving in a more temperate season. He feared that any delay might simply provide time for doubts or other conflicts to throw him off track. In France, at least, this proved to be a blessing. As he explained to me, "first of all, the dull plains became this astonishing winter landscape... It was like I was walking through an arctic wilderness. It was very, very beautiful." And second, thanks in part to the absence of other pilgrims in those months, "the amount of kindness and of hospitality I was shown was I expect far more than I could have anticipated if I'd walked six months later."[8]

This early experience upended Guy's expectations for the pilgrimage. Whereas he had anticipated a mostly internal experience, the abundance of generous hospitality "meant that almost every single night I met a stranger. And because I speak fairly good French, I was able to talk to them, to learn about their lives. Very quickly, this became the focus of my interests, learning more about the lives of the believers that I was staying with." Each night, Guy connected with kindness and plumbed the minds of the faithful. And each day after, he writes, "I walked with a warm sense of gladness, for it seemed possible to cross an entire country on charity alone."

*   *   *   *   *

Dwindling religious affiliation and engagement generates some negative social consequences which we have yet to properly confront.

As we've already seen in *Bowling Alone*, Robert Putnam focused primarily on the declining sources and expressions of social capital in the USA.[9] In discussing how this phenomenon plays out in American churches, he also anticipated similar problems that would trickle outward as a consequence of the broader shift away from religious engagement. "Churches," Putnam explains, "provide an important incubator for civic skills, civic norms, community interests, and civic recruitment. Religiously active men and women learn to give speeches, run meetings, manage disagreements, and bear administrative responsibility." Faith-based organizations have a disproportionately positive impact on the communities in which they operate, promoting skills and habits which generate value in many different contexts.

Jesse Graham and Jonathan Haidt extended Putnam's work by highlighting the importance of viewing religion "as a complex social system with many social functions, one of which is to bind people together into cooperative communities organized around deities."[10] Haidt's earlier definition of moral systems is also instructive here: "interlocking sets of values, virtues, norms, practices, identities, institutions, technologies, and evolved psychological mechanisms that work together to suppress or regulate selfishness and make social life possible." Putting it together, religions, as moral systems, help to engineer functional societies by promoting cooperation as a value *and* as a skill set.

This manifests in a number of distinct ways but two deserve special attention. First, religious people are, on par, happier than the general population. Arthur Brooks, author of *Gross National Happiness*, does not equivocate on this point: "There is an immense amount of data on this subject, and it indicates conclusively that religious people really are happier and better off emotionally than their secular counterparts."[11] But why? Graham and Haidt acknowledge arguments which claim the belief systems themselves contribute to this, offering some balm for the general anxiety we face as humans, but they then conclude that "most of the well-being benefits of religiosity appear to come from participation in a religious congregation." In arriving at that judgment, they highlight a study conducted by Ed Diener and Martin Seligman (2002), which demonstrated that, "when social relationships are controlled for, religiosity shows no unique prediction of well-being."[12] Religion provides the setting in which the community can come together, but the happiness emerges from the communal connection.

Second, religious communities consistently demonstrate increased charitable activity relative to other groups. Religious people consistently give more money and time to charitable causes, and Brooks explains that this "persists when controlling for education, age, gender, income, and political ideology." Steven Monsma takes it even farther, concluding that "religionists live out more facets of civic responsibility than do the irreligious."[13] While some argue that this is a case of "reputation management" by believers, Graham and Haidt challenge such claims and instead assert that "participation in a moral community that explicitly values charity and selflessness increases charitable behavior." Membership in a community with normalized values leads to the internalization and practicing of those values.

Perhaps I should remind the reader at this point that I am agnostic; I've never ascribed to a particular religious identity. Whereas that orientation was originally one of opposition, today it is merely one of absence. Regardless, I have no dog in this fight, nor any sort of proselytizing objective. I recognize, of course, the harm perpetrated by certain religious leaders, officials, and belief systems; there are excellent reasons that some harbor animosity for organized religion. There is a risk, though, of throwing out the belief with the bathwater. Religion brings us together in some fundamentally valuable ways for which we have yet to find many viable alternatives.

*   *   *   *   *

Michael Wolfe wasn't looking for a new religion. Rather, as he explains in *The Hadj: An American's Pilgrimage to Mecca*, "I wanted something to soften my cynicism. I was searching for new terms by which to see."[14] As a young man, he traveled to northern Africa, ostensibly for the thrill of adventure that accompanies novel experiences. While there, though, he had an experience somewhat akin to Malcolm X's at Mecca, seeing people of all different backgrounds coming together as Muslims.

Most of his peers at home were skeptical of organized religion; they viewed it as "political manipulation, or they dismissed it as a medieval concept." Wolfe wasn't moved by such arguments and refused to approach belief as a zero-sum game. Instead, he explains, "I wanted clarity and freedom. I did not want to trade away reason simply to be saddled with a dogma."

After that initial exposure to Islam, he spent ten years pondering conversion before finally making the leap, just a year before he began planning his pilgrimage. He would first journey to Morocco, where he had previously lived and traveled, and would observe Ramadan there, fasting among his fellow faithful. He would then carry on to Mecca.

Michael approached his first Ramadan as a Muslim with trepidation, anticipating the discomfort that would come from so many days of strict fasting. Nonetheless, the decision to spend it in Morocco proved pivotal: "From dreading the fast at home, I had come to like it in Morocco. If misery loves company, I had a whole country behind me. Even on the streets I found support." This specific social context transformed the experience from an ordeal into an act of collective sacrifice in service to a higher purpose.

*   *   *   *   *

The consequences of religious decline are not merely mundane or practical; they are also existential. We crave meaning and are all too vulnerable to despair and self-destructive behavior when bereft of it.

96

Viktor Frankl understood the perils of meaninglessness. In *Man's Search for Meaning*, he reflected on his experience as a prisoner in Auschwitz.[15] Even then, in the worst circumstances imaginable, he recognized that the "way in which a man accepts his fate and all the suffering it entails, the way in which he takes up his cross, gives him ample opportunity—even under the most difficult circumstances—to add a deeper meaning to his life." When a prisoner lost belief in the possibility of a better future, Frankl explained, they "became subject to mental and physical decay." Every prisoner feared that moment.

After one particularly bad day—an alarming distinction in an extermination camp—Frankl and his fellow prisoners lay in their rooms, teetering on the brink of total despair. Recognizing the peril, Frankl spoke to them. "I told my comrades (who lay motionless, although occasionally a sigh could be heard) that human life, under any circumstances, never ceases to have a meaning, and that this infinite meaning of life includes suffering and dying, privation and death. I asked the poor creatures who listened to me attentively in the darkness of the hut to face up to the seriousness of our position. They must not lose hope but should keep their courage in the certainty that the hopelessness of our struggle did not detract from its dignity and its meaning."

Frankl appealed to their sense of connection to someone or something important: "I said that someone looks down on each of us in difficult hours—a friend, a wife, somebody alive or dead, or a God—and he would not expect us to disappoint him." He exhorted them to see that meaning also existed in their sacrifice and recalled the story of a comrade, "who on his arrival in camp had tried to make a pact with Heaven that his suffering and death should save the human being he loved from a painful end. For this man, suffering and death were meaningful; his was a sacrifice of the deepest significance." Only with this orientation, Frankl believed, could they endure the nightmare of the Holocaust.

Frankl survived and subsequently made a tremendous impact in his field of psychotherapy by introducing the concept of logotherapy, which builds on his belief in the critical importance of meaning. When writing *Man's Search for Meaning*, he observed that many of his patients suffered from an "existential vacuum," which he characterized as "the feeling of the total and ultimate meaninglessness of their lives. They lack the awareness of a meaning worth living for. They are haunted by the experience of their inner emptiness, a void within themselves." This was a distinctly modern phenomenon; Frankl argues that "the traditions which buttressed [human] behavior are now rapidly diminishing." Without those externalized sources of comfort to provide viable sources of meaning, humans have become increasingly shiftless, lost, and depressed. Unable to fulfill our "will to meaning," as Frankl calls it, many compensate by transforming it into a will to power, or money, or pleasure—none of which can properly fill the void.

Another existential theorist, Ernest Becker, inspired a psychological framework that is equally relevant to the discussion: Terror Management Theory (TMT). Developed by Sheldon Solomon, Jeff Greenberg, and Tom Pyszczynski, TMT originates from humanity's uniquely fraught reality—we are the only creatures alive that are cognizant of our own mortality. Knowing that we are doomed to die, regardless of our efforts, generates intense anxiety. Fortunately, our intellect—which got us into this mess to begin with—also offers a way out. As the three scholars explain in *The Worm at the Core*, "Our shared *cultural worldviews*—the beliefs we create to explain the nature of reality to ourselves—give us a sense of meaning, an account for the origin of the universe, a blueprint for valued conduct on earth, and the promise of immortality."[16]

That's a mouthful and requires some parsing. Starting at the end, TMT recognizes that the shortest route to managing anxiety over mortality involves replacing it with immortality. Unfortunately, science has yet to cooperate on that front. Instead, many humans rely on the promise of literal immortality that some religions offer. Sure, the thinking goes, we might die here and now, but there's something better (for some of us!) on the other side. And that belief certainly helps. It's one reason why religion remains important for us today. However, religion isn't the only way to mitigate anxiety over our encroaching mortality; it's also possible to promote a kind of *symbolic* immortality, by attaching ourselves to a cultural identity that will endure. For example, even if I don't ascribe to a religious belief, I can see myself as an American, and I can tell myself—as I'm often reminded—that I belong to the "greatest country on God's green earth." Even though I will inevitably die, my country and culture, I have to believe (even if it sometimes feels at odds with available evidence), will survive and excel. But here's the catch: it works most effectively only if I live a life that meets and even exceeds the standards that exist in the USA for what constitutes a *good* life, or a life of value. My self-esteem and the effectiveness of my coping with death anxiety both depend upon how successfully I've reached what American culture deems worthy.

This is doubly unfortunate. First, it relies on being able to follow a set of cultural values that are healthy, inclusive, and *possible*. A quick review of how we define beauty in the USA will expose one particular place in which we fall short of those goals. Second, it often generates conflict, as we tend to reinforce the security of our own cultural affiliations by asserting the inferiority of others. Acknowledging these dire challenges, Solomon and his colleagues write, "we need to fashion worldviews that yield psychological security… but also promote tolerance and acceptance of ambiguity." If we are unable to maintain a strong faith in our culture, or if we worry that we fall short of our culture' standards of success and goodness, we become particularly vulnerable to existential despair.

Frankl postulates that many of the most common manifestations of mental illness that we face today—ranging from depression to addiction to aggression—were shaped in part by an underlying existential vacuum. In his study of depression, *Lost Connections*, Johann Hari made a similar discovery.[17] Synthesizing research conducted all over the world, Hari writes that "the more materialistic and extrinsically motivated you become, the more depressed you will be." The problem is not solely that we strive to meet cultural norms—though intrinsically motivated people are, in fact, consistently happier. Rather, Hari explains, "We are being propagandized to live in a way that doesn't meet our basic psychological needs—so we are left with a permanent, puzzling sense of dissatisfaction." Far too many of us are bound to "an incorrect set of values telling [us] to seek happiness in all the wrong places."

To be greater, we require *something* greater—a source of meaning that inspires hope and tempers anxiety, that promotes healthy values we can strive toward and acceptance of difference. In many of our countries and cultures, at least some of the dominant values miss the mark badly.

*   *   *   *   *

"Mon ami, do you think the [hajj] begins in Mecca? No, no. It starts the moment you decide to go. Forget itineraries! The only itinerary is *al-sirat*."

As Michael prepared to travel from Morocco to Saudi Arabia, he received guidance from the many experienced pilgrims around him. While many offered very specific advice on the exact course he should follow on hajj and precisely how many days he should spend in each location, his friend Medhi counseled him to remain focused on the cornerstone of his faith. In Islam, *al-sirat* or *Sirat-al-Mustaqim* refers to the "straight" or "right" path, the way of living that pleases Allah.

Michael didn't struggle with most aspects of Islam; he took to the faith and its practices quite smoothly. However, he had a difficult time accepting the idea behind *insha'Allah*. Muslims affix the phrase, which literally translates to "God willing," to any statement that anticipates the future; it acknowledges that their lives are in God's hands.

This notion chafed against Michael's hardwired orientation to strive for control in any circumstance. He reflects that "this deep provisionality of Islam challenged my most ingrained Western reflex: to look ahead, to cover my back, to live with one foot in the future." Instead of trying to anticipate every step of his pilgrimage, Michael needed to surrender himself to the experience.

Once in Saudi Arabia, that process became much easier. At the airport—technically the world's largest at that point, in 1990, in terms of overall area covered—he was immersed in a crowd of Muslims from all over the world, with a new jumbo jet disgorging believers every five minutes. Every woman wore white kaftan robes and scarves; every man wore the ihram. This marked a transformative moment for Michael: "The ihram had a powerful impact on me, too. For one thing, it put an end to my months of arrangements. In a way it put an end to me as well. The uniform cloth defeats class distinctions and cultural fashion. Rich and poor are lumped together in it."

Michael and his cohort proceeded directly to the Kaaba. He sets the scene: "The core of the mosque at [Mecca] is on the round, an open, roofless forum overlooked by tiered arcades. The marble floor is 560 feet on the long sides, 350 feet wide, and polished to the whiteness of an ice rink. At the center of this hub stands the [Kaaba], a four-story cube of rough granite covered in a black embroidered veil." The mere act of arrival ignited waves of emotion in the burgeoning crowd. "Men wept and muttered verses where they stood. Women leaned against columns, crying the rarest sort of tears—of safe arrival, answered prayers, gratified desire. I shared these emotions."

They weren't in attendance to simply observe, though. Michael and his fellow Muslims proceeded to engage in the tawaf, or turning, which involved completing a series of circuits around the hub, saluting the ancient monolith and praising Allah throughout. Initially, they moved swiftly, at a pace that surprised Michael: "I had not imagined the [hajj] would be so athletic." After the first three circuits, though, the believers slowed and Michael absorbed more of the ritual; he learned which phrases to shout, to join his voice with his fellows, and he admired the Kaaba. Finally, near the end, the experience coalesced in Michael's mind: "One had to perform the tawaf to comprehend it... Orbiting shoulder to shoulder with so many others induced in the end an open heart and a mobile point of view." An act of interpersonal synchronization, if ever there was one.

Joined together in so many ways—in dress, movement, message, and belief—Michael already found himself unified with his fellow Muslims. Back in Morocco, his mentor Abd al-Qadir had presciently told him not to worry about the crowds on pilgrimage. "Things will be elbow to elbow, but that's how one makes friends... The [hajj] diminishes people's self-importance. It shrinks their egos to peanuts. You will see."

Abdellah's transition into Saudi Arabia was more turbulent. As he neared Medina, where his pilgrimage would begin, he anxiously anticipated what he might encounter there. His attempt to explore that uncertainty with a fellow passenger failed miserably; the passenger "made no effort to hide his surprise, and let me know brusquely that our conversation was at an end." This left Abdellah feeling "doubly alone." After hours on the road, Abdellah was shuffled off with a group for processing, an experience in which he felt treated like "a piece of merchandise, a mere pilgrim and nothing else, denuded of any other identity." This transformative process of becoming a pilgrim, which had felt uplifting and unifying for Michael, proved dehumanizing for Abdellah.

Nonetheless, they traveled to the Prophet's Tomb. Abdellah observed the procession like the detached anthropologist studying a phenomenon, and concluded that the pilgrims "were in search not of the deepening of their ideas or theories about divine or human nature, about revelation or the afterlife, a sum of beliefs or evidence, but, rather, of the deepening (if one has to use the term) of their faith." Abdellah's hajj, by contrast, was inspired by that first category of motivations, which only reinforced his distance from his peers. Nonetheless, he finally pushed himself forward, into the immediate proximity of the tomb. The effect was profound. "This flash of intuition projected all around me the light and contrasts of an open clearing. I felt a joy like no joy I had felt before. I had rediscovered a specific humanity at last."

Two days later, still in Medina, Abdellah and his companions rose early to pray. Arriving at the mosque, suddenly immersed in an "enormous crowd," he "was seized by a feeling of religious fear." This wasn't just religious panic; it was a full-blown identity crisis. "Who was this person who'd been suddenly taken over and possessed? Was the face I believed was mine crumbling in contact with prayer, with the ground?"

A similar phenomenon took place when Abdellah arrived at the Kaaba. From the sidelines, Abdellah witnessed the impassioned believers engaged in worship, and studied the ancient monolith, only to have his detached observations washed away by an upsurge of emotions. "Tears welled up in my eyes but didn't flow, putting me in tune with the others. I will never know, I am sure, with what these tears were associated, but I was experiencing something concrete and precise: I felt I had been stripped bare." This experience sparked sudden recognition within Abdellah; only now could he fully understand how other pilgrims could lay claim to happiness and joy here. And yet, that same experience reignited terror: "I couldn't rid myself of the sense of imminent punishment, of a plague that would suddenly arise and defeat me. This fear tortured me… It paralyzed me, gave me shudders."

Abdellah carried on with his hajj. He went through the motions. "I addressed and carried out the acts of worship respectfully. They bound me to others, to all the others." However, while physically present, his mind was often elsewhere, "in a state beyond myself that many would not have accepted and that would have triggered hostility, repression, or execution."

Michael and Abdellah made the same pilgrimage, visited the same sacred places, worshipped among equivalent crowds of believers. While Michael found comfort and connection in the physical experience, relinquishing his own personal concerns, Abdellah's were often amplified. Surrounded by Muslims in Mecca, he felt isolated, vulnerable, and unsafe.

*　　*　　*　　*　　*

While participation in organized religion declines across the developed world, we are simultaneously witnessing an increase of less formal manifestations of spirituality. Thus, despite a growing percentage of religiously unaffiliated people, scholars claim that we have actually moved past the "secular" era and entered a "post-secular" one.

Mats Nilsson and Tesfahuney Mekonnen offer a helpful introduction to post-secularism.[18] After years of scientific and technological progress, chipping away at religious traditions and undermining "the social significance and role of organized religion," post-secularism marks a reassertion of the importance of belief. Humanity, after all, abhors an existential vacuum. However, perhaps inspired by the aforementioned social breakdown, faith in the post-secular era has moved increasingly to the private and individual realms.

Crucially, Nilsson and Mekonnen continue, these post-secular religious interests diverge from more traditional manifestations. Whereas traditional "religious belief and practice is associated with the rituals, practices and traditions of churches and religious communities," today we observe "a kind of spiritual plurality, which focuses on the individual, private, faith and practice." The individual, not the community, stands at the center of this post-secular approach; the new religious orientation has more to do "with questions of existence, meaning and fulfillment" than "expectations and obligations." Paul Heelas and Linda Woodhead carry that point even farther: the shift from religion to spirituality, they assert, has resulted in "a life lived by reference to one's own subjective experiences" instead of a "life lived in terms of external or 'objective' roles, duties and obligations."[19]

This way of thinking about "post-secular religion" aligns with the rather amorphous concept of "spirituality," a term that requires some definitional clarity. Nilsson recommends Hans Urs van Balthazar's framing, in which he defines spirituality as "seeking truth and meaning through lived experience; using this experience to express and fulfil oneself in the world; and recognizing some higher power beyond oneself to guide one's thoughts and actions."[20]

At this point, it's important to stress that a post-secular, spiritualistic approach is not inherently negative! We need meaning and fulfillment, and in the face of religious decline, we've got to find it where we can. However, spirituality does risk functioning as a pale imitation of the more valuable original. Fruit juice is delicious and, while not ideal for every diet, it's worth enjoying on occasion. However, that juicing process strips the fruit of some of its most valuable nutrients. The feelings of satisfaction that accompany its consumption are thus often inconsistent with the actual value.

Religion elevates our lives by bringing us together. A totally individualized spirituality may lack that connective power.

*   *   *   *   *

Propelled forward by that "warm sense of gladness," Guy finished crossing France and proceeded into Switzerland. While the winter passage through France brought unexpected delights, it also posed serious hazards as Guy advanced into the Alps. The prevailing wisdom is that trekking over the historic Grand Saint Bernard Pass in that season is both impractical and a genuine threat to life and limb. Guy kept going.

The threat was not overstated. Iced-over bridges, trails long buried beneath snow, and freezing conditions all imperiled Guy as he climbed higher. Navigating several near-misses, his mind drifted back to those "dark nights of the depression." He recalled telling his doctor that he "felt defeated, and that this feeling of defeat was so overwhelming it made dying seem the simplest way to surrender." What stood out in hindsight was not the imminence of death, but rather "a sense of stunned isolation, though in fact I was rarely alone."

Guy survived. Reading his memoir, I struggled to understand what was going through his mind as he confronted such difficulty in the Alps, after already having faced despair back home. While he certainly wasn't consciously considering this in the moment, Guy explained to me that there was a direct line between those two moments. Walking through Switzerland proved profoundly instructive: "to be in a dangerous situation, and to find that you don't just give up, that you actually struggle and strive to stay alive, that was something that built my confidence as I carried on walking."

Having cleared the Alps, Guy descended into Italy, right on track for what had emerged as a major goal in his walk: to reach Rome by Easter Sunday. He marched unrelentingly southward, growing stronger with every step. His on-schedule arrival in Rome should have been a triumph, an accomplishment that would bolster his confidence as he continued onward. Instead, it was crushing.

Far from a "real" pilgrim, Guy felt exposed. "I was suddenly surrounded by real believers," he told me, "for whom the Easter narrative is not a pretty story or a series of interesting metaphors. For whom it's something that really happened. And I was suddenly aware of the gulf between what this meant to everyone around me and what this meant to me." At earlier points on his pilgrimage, Guy felt enriched by his exposure to and participation in Christian rituals. However, "when confronted with the services at their most spectacular, I actually felt that I was an impostor, an outsider, that I wasn't really meant to be there."

Instead of moving forward rejuvenated, Guy suddenly faced a crisis. He fled Rome, rejoining the pilgrim road, "but my sense of purpose was gone. If the ritual had no meaning, why keep going? Why not give up?"

*   *   *   *   *

While religious belief certainly functions as a key impetus for many pilgrims, it's the growing contingent of spiritually inclined people that has played the key part in the contemporary resurgence of walking pilgrimages.

Spain's Camino de Santiago exemplifies this trend. Research conducted by Suzanne Amaro and colleagues in 2015 revealed that two of the more "traditional" pilgrim motivations—religious inspiration and fulfilling promises—actually ranked at the bottom of their respondents' reasons for walking.[21] Instead, "spiritual motivations" were most popular, followed closely by the desire for "new experiences" and outdoor adventures. Whereas earlier studies asserted that pilgrims walked for religious purposes, the Camino's continued growth is built upon "a spiritual revolution."

The spiritual pilgrim has a particular approach. As Nilsson and Tesfahuney explain, post-secular pilgrims take pilgrimage's religious traditions and rework them in service to their own beliefs. Instead of buying the religious belief system wholesale, they tend "to 'pick up' bits and pieces and build-up a whole." As those pilgrims construct their own distinct experience, they also reshape the pilgrimage in their image. In the process, Nilsson and Tesfahuney assert, "the meaning and place identity of Santiago is gradually shifting from a place whose meaning is tied primarily to a collective religious identity into one that is fleeting, porous and personal or individualized."

Wutai Shan, a sacred Buddhist mountain in China, represents an excellent example of this a la carte approach to belief. The Chinese government banned religious practice during the Cultural Revolution (1966-76), and while it was technically permitted once more following reforms in 1978, worship often remained a private affair.

As Robert Shepherd and colleagues explain, the dramatic changes unfolding in urban China over the past four decades of rapid modernization have prompted a search for meaning, for something lasting, among many Chinese.[22] This has not resulted in a surge of Chinese adopting religious identities; Xinzhong Yao estimates that only 5.3% of Chinese people self-identified as religious in 2005, and a mere 2.6% as Buddhist.[23] However, it has spurred an appreciable uptick in religious *practices*. More than half of

Wutai Shan's pilgrims "engaged in religious practices such as burning paper money and worshipping ancestors," while more than three-quarters "agreed with the fundamental Buddhist precept that 'goodness will have good recompense.'" The authors also conclude that religion in China has morphed to the point that, "Rather than serving as training sites for instructing people in 'how to be Buddhists', these temples enable the practice of Buddhism for people concerned with fate and fortune." The purpose has shifted from transcendent to pragmatic.

One of the most critical "bits and pieces" that the spiritually oriented individual has to "pick up" is personal ritual. Tatjana Schnell and Sarah Pali explain how these practices, traditionally fulfilled through religious mechanisms, remain critical for meaning making.[24] This holds true in particular on the Camino. Whether motivated by formal religious belief, more generalized spirituality, or purely secular objectives, Schnell and Pali found that pilgrims benefited from their walk. "Directly after the journey as well as four months later, pilgrims experience life as significantly more meaningful, and crises of meaning have been overcome. Independently of the original motives, the majority of pilgrims experience the journey as transformative in a constructive sense."

If a shift from a religious orientation to a more spiritual one risks exacerbating the modern existential vacuum, pilgrimage offers a clear approach to filling that void by re-connecting the pursuit of meaning with a communal context.

*   *   *   *   *

Unlike Guy's steady march south, Timothy's pilgrimage stumbled onward in fits and starts. He struggled to get into a walking flow. He suffered a troublesome leg injury and endured serious blisters. For a time, he even had to suspend his pilgrimage in Switzerland to return home, as a loved one received cancer treatment. Nothing about his experience proceeded smoothly or as planned.

Back in the United States, Timothy reflected that "my heart, head, and soul never left the [Via Francigena]. I missed being a pilgrim." He later returned to Switzerland and, if anything, his pilgrimage became even choppier. He bused to the Grand Saint Bernard Pass because of poor weather. He took an uber and train through the Piedmont due to bad feet. When those ailments persisted, he opted to rent a car to carry him onward to Tuscany.

Despite these physical misfortunes, the internal journey continued. Timothy's pilgrimage wouldn't ultimately inspire a definitive reconciliation with the Church; "I may never forgive his church," he reflected, "and [Pope Francis's] church may never be mine again." In lieu of that, though, it offered clarification: "the closer I get to Rome, the less cluttered my thinking." Timothy wasn't blessed with a miracle cure for his sister-in-law's cancer, but he came to appreciate the humility of praying for it. He couldn't explain why bad things happen to good people, but he eventually recognized that "it's futile to accept an ordered design to events." Most notably, Timothy realized, "I believe in the Resurrection, and I owe this sentiment to the Via Francigena." His religious identity remained fragile, but his faith would endure, a credit to the daily experience of pilgrimage.

That final epiphany signaled the end of Timothy's pilgrimage. After his third day in Rome, he, like Guy, became burned out on the city and ready to leave. He recognized, at that point, that his experience diverged from that of many of his pilgrim predecessors. "Millions who came before me believed they'd been given absolution for their sins, and went home with a clean soul. They got their passage to eternity. My return ticket is not such an easy one-way. I've resolved some things, but other matters will have to remain irresolvable. At the least, I know this: What I discovered was not served in a stiff shot. A stiff shot doesn't last." Instead of a "stiff shot" or certainty, Timothy's pilgrimage brought him "a conviction, this pilgrim's progress: There is no way. The way is made by walking."

Timothy flew home; Guy kept going.

*   *   *   *   *

Spiritually motivated pilgrimages certainly can, as Nilsson and Tesfahuney argued, morph a communally oriented religious experience into a more individualized one. In her study of pilgrims to Lourdes and Rocamadour, France's two most visited Catholic shrines, Deana Weibel examined the discrete experiences of two kinds of pilgrims: Catholics and "Religious Creatives."[25] She defined the latter as people whose belief systems are "mystical, eclectic, intentionally syncretic, highly personalized and experiential," so they certainly fall under the broader "spiritual" umbrella. Religious Creatives, Weibel explained, find value in pilgrimage destinations across all religious traditions, believing them to be imbued with an "energy" that aligns with the sacred or numinous.

We've already seen the extraordinary potency of the community of believers at Lourdes. Even in the absence of completely miraculous cures, many Catholic pilgrims have described being uplifted by the experience of being surrounded by so many kind and hopeful peers. Weibel saw the allure of *communitas* among Catholic pilgrims in her study as well. The Religious Creatives, however, functioned very differently. Placing a "high priority on the freedom associated with their spirituality," they operate individualistically, and "communitas [thus] appears to be a much less important motivation." Weibel highlighted one Religious Creative's pursuit of healing at Rocamadour through "basking," which involved "sitting passively in the Chapelle de Notre-Dame and receiving and being transformed by the energy that flowed into her." Both the Catholics and Religious Creatives in Weibel's study found fulfilling experiences on pilgrimage, but they achieved that in distinctly different ways.

Spiritually motivated pilgrimages do not, however, have to be individualistic enterprises. Even Nilsson and Tesfahuney acknowledge this point, writing that "during their stay in Santiago de Compostela, pilgrims are 'socialized' and become part of a temporary, pilgrim [community] with shared ways of being, feeling and acting that downplay their individual peculiarities and identities."

Indeed, one need only flip back to the previous chapter to see the many ways that pilgrims on the Camino de Santiago, regardless of their motivation, are galvanized into a larger whole. The near-universality of the "pilgrim family" experience, in which individual pilgrims on the Camino almost spontaneously coalesce into clans of companionship, shines through most Camino testimonials.

In this way, the appeal of pilgrimage to spiritually minded people strikes me as encouraging. Regardless of an underlying individual impulse, the call to pilgrimage, I would assert, is also inspired by the urgency of finding one's flock. Pilgrims seek a community of seekers, a fertile field in which their own beliefs can be nurtured and grow strong. Even if every pilgrim has a distinct spiritual destination in mind, the journey is nonetheless one that can be made together.

In their discussion of the healing potential of pilgrimage, Jill Dubisch and Michael Winkelman note that pilgrimage can "restore one's relationships with aspects of the sacred" through a process that is both healing and "whole-ing."[26] Those words are linked, etymologically, through "the common Indo-European linguistic roots of *holy, whole,* and *heal.*" While their focus leans more toward the process of making ourselves psychologically whole through a deeper connection with the divine, our social fracturing also demands repair. Pilgrimage offers a setting in which we can strive for both spiritual and social wholeness.

* * * * *

Abdellah had come to Mecca spiritually fractured. While his Muslim culture shaped the foundations of his identity, Islamic religion had long represented a source of anxiety and even fear for him. The initial days of his hajj had done little for this.

Leaving Mecca, pilgrims travel some 20km through Mina to Mount Arafat. Arafat is imbued with layers of meaning. Believed to be the site of Muhammad's farewell speech to his fellow hajjis near his life's end, it is also known as the Mount of Mercy, the place where Adam and Eve were united after the Fall and forgiven by God. Abdellah describes it as a place that "touches primordial innocence: birth. The pilgrimage washes away all sin; one emerges from it purified, 'just like a newborn baby.'"

The experience of communal prayer near Arafat made a significant impact on Abdellah. "I could feel deep within me the astonishing energy of a worshipping people: dedicated, devout, devoted...These were moments of rest, moments of meditation that returned us to ourselves and turned us inwards."

If Abdellah's experience in Mecca, surrounded by devout faithful, had sometimes generated feelings of anxiety and impostor syndrome, the journey to Arafat and back to Mecca helped to break down some of those barriers. "The very real emotion that brought me into close proximity with pilgrims, all absorbed in accomplishing a spiritual project, resulted from a promised reunion 'between thought and motion.'" Something ancient was at work—a primal association between movement and the mind that proved freeing for Abdellah. "I was discovering my existence anew," he realized, and "this fresh discovery, which grew clearer with each of the hajj's walks and stations, showed me myself in an utterly new light."

Leaving Mecca, Abdellah recognized that the hajj had "led me to another crossroads," one that would spur him to "search for a way to re-create myself." His memoir offers no definitive conclusion, no redefining clarity, as the transformation continued to unfold as he wrote the final pages. However, his expectations had been upended. After believing he could complete the hajj as an anthropologist, as a detached observer, the "dynamism" of the experience roped him in. Immersed in so many distinct elements—"the coming together with no other objective than the rite, the sites with their eschatological charge, the dramas superimposed on them day and night, the prayers, the circumambulations, the strolls"—he found that "there was always more to hear in what was said, more to see in what was seen, more to contemplate in what was thought."

Like Timothy with Catholicism, the pain Abdellah carried from his past with Islam hadn't suddenly disappeared. That burden persisted. However, it was accompanied now by the enriching emotions that arose from a deeply meaningful experience that linked Abdellah with a community, *his* community, of believers.

*   *   *   *   *

The power of pilgrimage to bolster a shared identity is exemplified not just by established pilgrimage traditions, like the Camino de Santiago and Hajj, but perhaps even more so by newly developed pilgrimages that forge closer ties along religious, national, and ideological lines.

As we've seen, the Indian sub-continent has a rich pilgrimage tradition. Within that context, however, Sikhism stands out as an exception. As Dallen Timothy and Daniel Olsen explain, "pilgrimage is not prescribed in Sikh scriptures and is in fact commonly discouraged."[27] Indeed, "Sikh scriptures clearly state that pilgrimage is meaningless, that it is more important to have a pure mind and lead a truthful life." Sikh Gurus promoted what they claimed to be a more rational approach, arguing that people don't need to travel great distances to find a connection with the divine.

And yet, Sikhs do participate in pilgrimage, visiting a whole host of different sacred places, most notably the Golden Temple at Amritsar. They are commonly drawn to places of great importance to Sikh history; visiting such places helps to connect them with Sikh cultural and spiritual traditions. Certainly, they take the opportunity to pray for positive outcomes—happiness, good health, prosperity—but the deeper motivation is one of connection. As the authors conclude, Sikh pilgrimage sites "play a vital role in creating a sense of community among its members."

While Jewish tradition included a more prominent role for pilgrimage, Mara Cohen Ioannides and Dimitri Ioannides argue that it has shifted markedly over time.[28] Instead of its more traditional manifestations, the most common forms of Jewish pilgrimage today are best described as "nostalgic pilgrimages." Jewish nostalgic pilgrimages are characterized by "the need to visit a place influenced by a strong yearning to connect with one's history," a similar impulse to what we just witnessed in contemporary Sikhism. This yearning is particularly pronounced among Jewish people because of two main factors—the far-reaching Jewish diaspora, scattered so far from its ancestral homeland, and a shared history that is rife with tragedy.

Despite their geographic fragmentation, Ioannides and Ioannides explain, Jews have sustained "an underlying belief in unity" and this, in turn, inspires an impulse to "travel Jewishly." The latter includes visiting sites of Jewish heritage and history, or with a particular Jewish purpose." For many Jews, travel to places associated with Jewish communities destroyed in the Holocaust is an essential experience. As Dallen Timothy explains, these nostalgic pilgrimages often include two elements: a personal pilgrimage to the site of a community that one's family once inhabited, along with a communal pilgrimage to an extermination or concentration camp.[29] Despite the distinction, the combined experience, while not explicitly religious, nonetheless forges a connection to their shared Jewish tradition.

The popular resurgence of pilgrimage in Norway is particularly surprising, given that the tradition was largely eradicated within the country. As Lisbeth Mikaelsson explains, the Lutheran Church "abolished pilgrimage and [the] cult of saints in 1536, in the wake of the Reformation."[30]

Nonetheless, the historic pilgrimage route associated with Saint Olav, linking Oslo and Trondheim, has been recovered in painstaking detail, among a network of other trails and sites. While many Norwegians still maintain a technical affiliation with the Church of Norway, the pilgrimage impulse is driven to a large degree by post-secular motivations. "[T]he desire to feel connected to the traditions of one's ancestors," Mikaelsson writes, "has become apparent as a contemporary identity issue having spiritual overtones." Despite participating in a Christian pilgrimage and maintaining an affiliation with a Christian church, Norwegian pilgrims are drawn more to the act by a desire for a deeper connection with their national and cultural traditions.

Beyond religious, cultural, and national affiliations, pilgrimage also offers the possibility of a deeper engagement with gender identity. In her discussion of the Goddess Movement, a modern Pagan pilgrimage phenomenon, Kathryn Rountree describes the importance for many participants of encountering ancient artifacts of Goddess worship traditions.[31] She argues that "such journeys contribute to a radical re-inscription of the female body by exposing women pilgrims to alternative representations of the feminine and by providing contexts in which the feminine can be re-imagined and re-experienced through symbolic activity and ritual." Whereas most pilgrimages are linked to particular cultural contexts, the Goddess Movement is far-reaching, cutting across ancient practices in Europe, Asia, Africa, and the Americas, appealing to more universal traditions and a broader source of connection.

Pilgrim testimony speaks, as well, to the healing and relief received from these experiences. One pilgrim highlighted the positive impact that Goddess observance had on her body image: "faced with these extraordinary fat figures I found myself unable to be objective at all. They simply delighted me. Their size moved me. They filled me with a joy in the beauty of my own body that I have never felt before." This was a transformative personal experience, inspiring a change in self-perception. Other pilgrims speak to a larger mission: "We seek to heal the wounds of patriarchy, violence and war. We hope to participate in the creation of ecologically balanced, peaceful cultures in which every woman and man, every creature and every living thing is respected and revered for its unique contribution to the web of life." In this way, the Goddess Movement functions as both a sacred act and an expression of a higher calling, a pilgrimage both nostalgic and aspirational.

Sikhs, Jews, Norwegians, women: all found a connection to something greater through these pilgrimages, even if—in most cases—they were not traditionally religious acts.

*   *   *   *   *

Of course, for Michael, his pilgrimage to Mecca was an explicitly religious act—and an obligatory one, to boot. It was an act he performed joyously, whole-heartedly, and largely free of internal conflict. Whereas Timothy and Abdellah sought some form of faith rehabilitation on their pilgrimages, Michael's hajj was an earnest celebration of his decision to convert to Islam.

Returning toward Mecca from Arafat, Michael reflected on the journey. The hajj, he realized, was "not a destination… but a direction" and in that it "remained true to life's inexorable motion." You didn't go "to" hajj, but rather "on" it; you "arrived to go." The hajj's significance, Michael thought, came not from an ethical function, as Islam's other four pillars did, but rather as "a turning point, a rite of passage accomplished on two feet." He realized that, for "all its public aspects the experience was intensely personal." Immersed in crowds for days on end, constantly in motion and often exhausted, Michael still recognized that an internal process of transformation was unfolding. At the same time, it was undoubtedly "a shared rite of passage," one in which he saw "through the eyes of others as much as through my own. In that way it was like an act of love." The dual journeys, internal and external, personal and social, were mutually reinforcing, working in tandem to amplify the sacredness of the experience.

If he initially struggled with releasing himself to the will of Allah, the pilgrimage offered fertile ground for growth in this realm. Late in his pilgrimage, Michael's group journeyed to Medina for a short visit. He went to the mosque for prayer and found it packed full of worshipers. "I enjoyed keeping in step with the congregation. It was part of the secret of the [hajj]—that the more chaotic events became, the less control you had to exert to get through them." By adhering to the rites, by relinquishing control, by joining the collective motion of the faithful, Michael came to understand the meaning behind *Insha'Allah*.

As seamless as his hajj had been in comparison to Abdellah's, Michael departed Mecca in a position that was not altogether different. "Whereas the [hajj] is a culmination for most pilgrims, he reflected, it felt more like a starting point to me." This was not a conclusion; it, too, was a crossroads. For Michael, the pilgrimage was "a vivifying factor," a spark to ignite his religious life, transforming it from one of two-dimensional observance to a vibrant and dynamic experience. Pilgrimage had revealed what was possible, but only in its aftermath would Michael be able to fully internalize its meanings.

*　　*　　*　　*　　*

Michael's hajj offers an important reminder: while acknowledging the pronounced increase in spiritually minded pilgrims, we shouldn't lose sight of the fact that pilgrimage remains a most effective conduit through which an individual can deepen and intensify their relationship with the divine. When Alice Warrender set out on pilgrimage on the Via Francigena, like Guy she was recovering from an extended period of brokenness.

In writing her memoir, *An Accidental Jubilee*, Alice had to rely on her parents' account of what went wrong, because she was out cold at the time.[32] She had crashed her bike, fallen unconscious, and ended up in a London hospital. To the extent that one can be lucky in such circumstances, the label fits Alice, as she was only found and treated because paramedics were already in the area, attending to a heart attack victim. One keen-eyed paramedic spotted her, lying in the wreckage of her bike. The doctors discovered an extradural hematoma, performed five hours of brain surgery to remove it, and thus set in motion a two-year recovery for Alice with an uncertain prognosis. She was informed, quite simply, that "the mental outcome... was uncertain, and all that could be advised was careful consideration of life ongoing."

Alice slept through most of the first three months of recovery. A short journey to a bookstore in month four kindled an interest, something to think about as she gingerly nursed her body back: the pilgrim roads to Rome. In the weeks ahead, Alice secretly learned about the Via Francigena, gradually concocting a plan, somehow balancing realism and optimism. "I knew that I was in no fit state to walk to Rome," she reflected, "but I believed I could get there." Remarkably, from lying incapacitated in a hospital bed in mid-February, she was cleared for pilgrimage in late-June and in Canterbury on July 12, ready to begin her journey.

Alice's pilgrimage began with joy and gratitude. She reveled in the day's walk, in all its imperfection: "I began to feel the cocoon of my own world forming. I passed so much today, leaving a city down a dreary canal, making a friend in the only village I passed through, and learning how it really feels to be lost and alone. I am so happy." Her early successes restored some measure of self-confidence and helped Alice believe that she could regain what she had lost through her injury. She also realized, though, that the pilgrimage served a higher calling. Her perspective on life had shifted fundamentally: "A sense of God is the only real thing that has got inside me since my accident. I know now that my life is not in my own hands and my fate is beyond my control." Sitting at mass in Laon, still early in her pilgrimage, she recognized that she walked for God, to acknowledge that she "owed it to him to show that I have the determination to live the life he has given me and in return I needed the time to work out where it was I went wrong."

Understandably, given that major brain surgery was not far behind her, Alice struggled physically at many points in her pilgrimage. Indeed, the suffering only seemed to intensify over the course of her journey southward. In Langres, France she "collapsed on the bed, feet throbbing, and cried and cried… wondering what on earth I was doing walking to Rome." Approaching Monteriggioni, Italy, she walked "just longing to get to the end of another day, reluctant to stop and rest for fear of it dragging on longer than it needs to." Near Torrenieri, Alice reached her nadir: "Not one bit of me was light or enjoying it. I felt tired, tired of the enormous effort to find pleasure in being in Italy and tired of the relentless walking with my belongings on my back along lonely dusty tracks with no other footprints."

Alice's internal turmoil kept pace with her physical ordeal. Fifty-three days into her pilgrimage, Alice fruitlessly strived "to work out what will challenge me the most while giving me a profession as well as a purpose for my existence." Early on, she worried that "it may be too late to embark on a new path," but that remained her goal throughout her walk. As on the Via Francigena, Alice believed that "inner happiness comes by remaining on one path and once the hard part has been conquered you reach a blissfully rewarding stage that you did not know was ahead of you." For Alice, that fulfilling purpose would only be made possible if she first completed her walk; quitting the latter would undermine the former.

Alice endured, buoyed by faith in God. Nearing the Swiss border with France, she realized that her earlier recognition that she walked her pilgrimage for God was helping her every day, supporting her through the most difficult moments. In Lucca, in a moment of particular vulnerability, she knew that there was "no way I could do it without believing in God."

As she finally approached Rome, Alice "lived, breathed and felt the beginnings of the intensity of complete peace awaiting me in St Peter's." Crossing into the Vatican, she experienced something cathartic: "I flung my arms in the air, my stick went up high, and the tears poured down my cheeks." Proceeding into the basilica, Alice "thanked God with a Mass under St Peter's in an intimate chapel of Our Blessed Lady of Czestochowa in the Vatican grottoes."

For all of the suffering along the way, God had seen Alice to Rome. "I walked with peace in my heart and belief in my soul." Alice found her path.

*   *   *   *   *

Seen as a whole, Alice's pilgrimage smacks of the miraculous—a fortunate discovery in London, a successful surgery, a smooth rehabilitation process, and the remarkable endurance required to complete a three-month walk almost fresh out of convalescence. It's the kind of incredible healing experience more commonly associated with Lourdes.

Despite that reputation, though, the overwhelming majority of pilgrims to Lourdes do not benefit from a divine cure for a physical illness or condition. While P.A. Morris's study reinforced that point, it also revealed something important.[33] Even without a cure, most of the pilgrims in the study demonstrated a "significant lessening" of anxiety and depression levels over the course of the year after the journey. The experience on pilgrimage, and particularly their time spent in Lourdes's thriving community of pilgrims, it turns out, "strengthened their religious faith, making it easier for them to live with their physical challenges."

Sometimes, a bolstered belief system *is* the miracle.

* * * * *

Guy lacked such conviction. His pilgrimage led him eastward now, crossing from Italy to Albania, then continuing on to Greece. The Easter disaster left him adrift and troubled, driving him deeper into dark thoughts. "I thought I could walk out the anger," he recalled, "but soon my heels were blistered, my legs burning." The whole experience was souring. "That anger was for the present as much as the past, because I knew this pilgrimage was no less childish: a wanton risk with my own well-being."

Struggling badly, Guy made a short detour to Mount Athos, an Eastern Orthodox monastic center that fills a peninsula in northeastern Greece. Now one among many pilgrims, Guy was drawn into the experience: "I enjoyed standing anonymous among these pilgrims. I realized it was not faith that made the mornings precious, but the patient practice of a ritual." He found relief in those moments. As he explained it to me, "there were occasional moments when I felt that I was temporarily moving outside of myself, or rather moving outside of the time-bound body that I usually inhabit, and therefore I would be able to close my eyes, let my mind drift, and 20 minutes or a half-hour would have passed."

Throughout his pilgrimage, Guy had found a certain appeal in monastic life. He was drawn to the notion of separating himself from the world and the strict structure supplied by ritual and routine. And yet, he also recognized the trap here, the perilous appeal of an escape from secular life to a young man who once attempted to escape his altogether. Instead, Guy left Mount Athos and continued onward. Nothing about the remainder of his journey would be smooth, but he would persist, walking through Turkey and Cyprus, Lebanon and Israel, and finally arriving in Jerusalem.

When Guy set out on this journey, he reflected, he "was bewitched by the stories of surrender, of sacrifice." Like monasticism, he thought at the time, religion offered "another way of leaving this life." Even if he no longer engaged in suicidal ideation, he recognized that, in his mind, death still offered "a release from shame, an escape from regret."

His pilgrimage experience, though, revealed a very different way of thinking about sacrifice. Indeed, it "could mean something much smaller: the habit of kindness, or the discipline of humility, or the steady practice of patience." Guy was reminded again of the charity he had received all along his pilgrimage—so many strangers coming through for him. Unlike Alice, Guy wasn't driven to walk for God; he made no claim to belief. However, as he shared with me, "if there was an act of faith on my own behalf, it was simply the process of walking and trusting that I would find these strangers and that they would look after me, and it was that act of faith which was the one that was rewarded."

"I thought I was walking into the wreckage of Christianity," Guy writes. On the contrary, he now realizes "how much remained." Instead of associating decline with inevitable demise, he surmised, perhaps it would be more accurate to see it as "evidence of endurance, and loss the price we pay for surviving." And if that was true for Christianity, perhaps it could be true for Guy as well.

Guy didn't suddenly convert to Catholicism or some other denomination of Christianity upon the conclusion of his pilgrimage. However, he emerged with a deeper perspective on religious faith. He shared his two new insights into belief with me. "The first insight was a fact that every anthropologist knows... religion is not really about a set of beliefs that you either do or don't believe. For most people it's about habits, traditions, communities, sense of identity—it's about all of the things that connect you to the other people who share in this faith, and maybe connect you to the world, or something beyond yourself."

Guy's second insight arose from his observation of many monks and nuns along the way. "The world is inherently or fundamentally mysterious, and religion is a way of entering that mystery more deeply... These are people who have dedicated their entire lives towards faith... and they're not founding that decision on some bulletproof certainty. They're actually founding it on a sense of uncertainty within which they can settle and within which they can endure potentially for an entire lifetime."

When Guy considered abandoning his pilgrimage after Rome, he spent a night in Anagni, Italy, where he was hosted by a young woman named Giulia. He told her about the Easter experiences and shared that he was struggling to figure out why to continue." After a pause, she described her decision to become a nun. She, too, had doubts; she, too, wondered if she was making the right choice. "I wish I was certain," she acknowledged, "like I always knew the future, but that means I wouldn't need God. He makes me brave when I'm afraid what happens next."

Guy carried this forward, a flash of wisdom that grew over the remainder of his pilgrimage. If offered him something essential. "It sounded hopeful and full of humility. As Giulia spoke, it seemed possible to doubt, possible to despair, yet still believe… There was courage here, born not from self-confidence but from living small before the world."

*   *   *   *   *

Pilgrimage affords us the rare opportunity to live our beliefs full-time, or to walk in the footsteps of another faith tradition, or to wrestle with our identity and beliefs in a more abstract sense. For Michael and Alice, pilgrimage reaffirmed the fit of their faith, while also exposing them to a deeper relationship with Allah and God respectively. For Timothy and Abdellah, the experience clarified questions. They weren't fully reconciled—both have experienced some of the most painful downsides of their respective religions, and those scars linger—but they found ways to redeem aspects of their beliefs and returned home with optimism. Guy found a way to live, by learning how to endure and appreciate uncertainty and through a renewed faith in his fellow humans.

As a teacher, I've come to appreciate the value of thoughtful and perceptive questions. Good questions provide a distinct lens or unique angle through which to make sense of the complex. They create possibilities. They don't point towards singular, easy answers; if they do, they're actually *terrible* questions. At their best, they inspire a productive ambivalence, a condition in which we revel in the pursuit of understanding a phenomenon. By contrast, clear answers close doors; they end conversations.

That uncertainty is easier to meet with steadfastness when we operate from a base of support, when we have a community behind us that is affirming, supportive, and kind, a community that provides us a sense of belonging. Faith becomes powerful and transformative, it becomes something greater, when it operates vertically and horizontally, linking us to the sacred and secular, the divine and the human. Pilgrimage is a setting in which we can richly experience both.

CONCLUSION

In the introduction to this book, I quickly walked back some of the title's rhetorical bombast. No, pilgrimage can't, in fact, solve *all* the problems we face in modern life. It certainly can't alleviate or eliminate some of the particularly complicated historical baggage that we bear.

It's for that reason that, several years ago, I grew uneasy with devoting a substantial amount of my life to pilgrimage. As my country became increasingly polarized, as global crises accelerated, as social injustices persisted in my own backyard, pilgrimage increasingly felt like pure, unadulterated self-indulgence and escapism. Blithely checking out from the news for five weeks every summer, especially lately, feels pretty good!

We have seen that pilgrimage can reconnect us with what really matters in life—to intrinsic motivations and prosocial values, to the natural world and the people around us. It breaks bad habits, interrupts vicious cycles, and offers the possibility of creating something better while finding something greater. And yet, like anything else, it can become watered down; it can all too easily become just another vacation. Intention matters.

But if a lack of intention can dilute pilgrimage, perhaps a more daring resolution can elevate the practice into something more transformative. And maybe, just maybe, my equivocation reflects a failure of imagination, more than any limitation inherent to pilgrimage.

*   *   *   *   *

Ian McIntosh, an anthropologist, had grown unsettled as well. After years spent working on justice and reconciliation initiatives in support of

Australia's aboriginal population, along with other global initiatives, he was assailed by doubts. As he told me, "I became downhearted with the lack of any real progress. Peace requires a major commitment to change," and yet that commitment proved lacking, time and time again.[1]

Before despair could take hold, though, Ian made a breakthrough: "I discovered the idea of pilgrimage and peacebuilding—places like Lebanon, India, and Ethiopia, and this really piqued my curiosity." After years of dead-ends, pilgrimage seemed to offer a way forward. "If people from different walks of life and different sides of the political and religious divide are already out there on the trail together," Ian asked himself, "could this be a foundation for peace work?"

He set out to answer that question. His international search led him, among other places, to Sri Lanka. The country endured a devastating civil war between 1983 and 2009, as a sustained armed conflict erupted between its Sinhalese/Buddhist majority and its Tamil/Hindu population. The tensions underlying that war were long-simmering, and hostilities have engulfed Sri Lanka's Muslim minority population as well. While peace has "prevailed" since 2009, Ian characterizes it as a "negative peace," which represents the "absence of conflict," as opposed to a "positive peace" that features "justice and bridge building."[2] Nonetheless, some efforts have been made to take tentative steps towards reconciliation, including a national goal of promoting interfaith connections.

Enter pilgrimage. Sri Lanka's most sacred site, "Sri Pada," draws believers of all faith traditions. Also known as "Adam's Peak" and the "Holy Footprint," its divine associations accrued over time, as new groups seized control of the island. Instead of becoming a source of division or a battleground for control, though, the peak brings together Sri Lankans of all backgrounds. "What's so startling about this pilgrimage site," Ian told me, "is that pilgrims of all these different faiths climb the mountain together, in their own style and at their own pace, often performing the very same rituals."

While those historic tensions persist elsewhere, only on Sri Pada and other pilgrimages do "the rigid boundaries between ethnicities and religious groups become porous. This porousness," Ian asserts, "can provide an avenue for achieving not only peace, but also reintegration and reconciliation."

When history pulls us apart, we struggle to find ways to bridge that gap. Pilgrimage can be that bridge.

*   *   *   *   *

Historical divisions plague Canada and New Zealand as well, particularly stemming from their tragic colonial legacies that have left indigenous populations in often dire circumstances, marked by disenfranchisement, marginalization, and trauma. That past marks those of settler ancestry as well, undermining well-intentioned attempts at reform. Much more thoughtful work is required to make reconciliation between these populations possible or productive. However, academic and religious innovators, in partnership and collaboration with indigenous leaders, are exploring the potential of pilgrimage to facilitate change in those countries as well.

In New Zealand, two Anglican priests, John Hornblow and Jenny Boyack, are spearheading this work.[3] The tradition of *hikoi*, which literally translates from the Maori language as "walks," but also has pilgrimage implications, is "a firmly embedded cultural understanding for Maori for whom purposeful walks or journeys were often to sacred or special places of meeting or encounter." Indeed, two prominent, nationwide *hikoi* inspired Hornblow and Boyack and shaped their understanding of social justice matters in New Zealand. The second of those proved particularly influential; "known as the Hikoi of Hope," it "saw approximately 40,000 people participating in local walks… to raise awareness of the suffering of the impoverished and disadvantaged."

Beginning in 2008, Hornblow and Boyack started to lead their own pilgrimages, specifically oriented toward bringing together Maori and Pakeha (people of European heritage) in a unifying experience. They have walked to key historical sites, places of great natural beauty, and to marae, or traditional Maori meeting places, where they have participated in formal ceremonies.

Meanwhile, in Canada, Matthew Anderson—a cleric and a professor—has sought to employ pilgrimage as part of a decolonizing process that allows settlers and First Nations people to explore their history and their relationship with the land. As part of a university program, he developed a short, two-day pilgrimage linking two traditional pilgrim sites: the Notre-Dame-de-Bons-Secours church in Old Montreal and Saint Kateri's shrine in Kahnawá:ke (Mohawk territory). The route spotlights the central role played by two revered women in the region: Saint Marguerite Bourgeoys, a French nun who founded the Notre Dame congregation in Montreal and later became Canada's first female saint, and Saint Kateri Tekakwitha, the first Native American woman in North America to be canonized. Anderson has also pursued longer reconciliatory pilgrimages through more rural parts of Canada, most notably on the North-West Mounted Police Patrol Trail in southern Saskatchewan.

Collectively, these pilgrimage initiatives in New Zealand and Canada provide walkers of European ancestry, in particular, with an opportunity to—in Anderson's words—"decolonize" themselves. As he told me, despite much conversation at a national level about reconciliatory progress, "Non-indigenous Canadians need to deal with the fact that we still have to deal with some truths before we can ever even approach the idea of reconciliation."[4] For Anderson, pilgrimage is a way for "those of us who are settler descendants, we learn about the land and we learn about the history of the land—in many cases, history that has been pushed aside and which we have never learned in school. And by learning about the land, we realize that the indigenous peoples who are resurgent in the Canadian West and are demanding more and more the rights that they signed for in treaty, that we learn something about our ongoing responsibilities to them."

Sometimes, those lessons are even more explicit. In the Kahnawá:ke pilgrimage, Anderson described how his group finally emerged from "this nitty-gritty graffiti-covered post-industrial part" of Montreal, and reveled in their emergence on the Saint Lawrence Seaway, a "beautiful treed area" that was a joy to walk through. When they arrived in Kahnawá:ke, though, the Mohawks they met commented that, "you know that bit of land that you were walking along, it was dredged up by expropriating Mohawk houses." The seaway could have been built on either side of the river, but settlers dominated the other side and rejected the idea wholesale, prompting the government to instead seize Mohawk lands. "By walking all of that, Anderson reflected, "we see how much land was taken away… and that the land can be beautiful, but still hide a terrible history."

For Hornblow and Boyack, meanwhile their pilgrimages "have been a way for a dominant people to move outside of their own cultural comfort zone; to build trusting and respectful relationships with *tangata whenua* (indigenous people or, literally, the people of the land); to experience vulnerability and discomfort; to view historic events through lesser-known narratives; and to have current values and practices challenged." By walking together—and designing the pilgrimage together, through a genuinely collaborative process—Hornblow, Boyack, and their Maori partners created opportunities for dialogue, discovery, and shared understanding. Facing this history directly, in a place-based and relationship-centered manner, plays a key part in the longer-term process of reconciliation.

*   *   *   *   *

Hornblow, Boyack, and Anderson have a bold vision for pilgrimage; William Ury's, by contrast, is downright audacious. The Middle East is perhaps the most complex and turbulent region in the world, fraught with historical tension and religious division. While the stories differ from place to place across the region, Ury realized, at the heart of those narratives was "the common experience of exclusion, trauma, and the desire of a people not to be further humiliated." And, at the heart of the region was one pivotal, shared narrative—that of Abraham, the shared forefather of Judaism, Christianity, and Islam. This became an inspiration for Ury. What if, he wondered, "a permanent pilgrimage route could be revived based on a commonality of cultures, rather than the conflict among them?"[5]

Thus, was born the Abraham Path. While it currently includes around 1000 kilometers of route through four Middle Eastern countries, it aspires, once fully developed, to cover five times that distance, through ten countries. For Ury, one of the world's foremost experts on high stakes negotiations, this was a peacebuilding initiative, one that sought to steer thinking in the region away from the "zero sum trap."

At the heart of the initiative stood the act of walking. First, it's an act of faith: "You go for a walk in the footsteps of Abraham. You retrace the footsteps of Abraham." But also, it's an action that occurs on common ground. "It's funny," Ury observed in a TED Talk, "when you walk, you walk side-by-side, in the same common direction. Now if I were to come to you face-to-face and come close to you, you would feel threatened. But if I walk shoulder-to-shoulder, even touching shoulders, it's no problem. Who fights while they walk?"[6]

It's not only the people you're walking with, though; it's the strangers encountered along the way. "How many of you have had the experience of being in a strange neighborhood or strange land, and a total stranger, perfect stranger, comes up to you and shows you some kindness—maybe invites you into their home, gives you a drink, gives you a coffee, gives you a meal? How many of you have ever had that experience? That's the essence of the Abraham Path." Indeed, when I followed the route through Palestine, each day's walk took me longer than expected as a direct consequence of farmers and shop-owners inviting me to join them for coffee.

Today, Nedal Sawalmeh lives in Nablus, Palestine and works as a guide on the Abraham Path. His parents relocated to a refugee camp north of Nablus from Jaffa, Israel in 1948, shortly after the State of Israel's founding. As Brian Mockenhaupt writes, Sawalmeh came to know the region well as a child, hiking through the hills and caves with friends, three of whom were killed in the Second Intifada.[7] That loss propelled him toward a life dedicated to peacebuilding. For Sawalmeh, the Abraham Path has the potential to support that objective. "Walking together creates a common understanding," he explains, adding that it's "a way of bringing people together as a first step." Instead of being caught in a binary conflict, he aspires to advance the conversation by being part of a "third side, to do something for peace."

Ury sees the Abraham Path as an opportunity to flip the script, to repurpose an old story for noble ends. "People learn through the stories that move them," he explains, "so if one could re-enter an old story, and retell it in a way that is relevant for today and tomorrow, it might be possible to begin to heal the old wounds."

We previously encountered Jill Dubisch's discussion of the importance of a new narrative for Vietnam War veterans, one that could promote healing by making "meaningful the confusing and traumatic experiences that often defied such meaning." So, too, do Hornblow, Ury, Boyack, and Sawalmeh seek to construct a more holistic and inclusive narrative, one that attends to past trauma while also creating space for the possibility of a shared future. And they see pilgrimage—walking together, side by side, through places of common heritage and history—as the place to tell that story together.

*   *   *   *   *

Beyond its reconciliatory and peace-building potential, pilgrimage also offers possibilities for mobilizing a response to the global threat of climate change. While that might sound like a stretch, the research highlights a pair of key contributions.

Our varied levels of environmental awareness and concern can be organized into three broad categories, courtesy of Stern and Dietz's framework.[8] "Egoistic" factors predispose a person to favor protections for parts of the environment that are of particular relevance to their lives, while disregarding others. That is, this inclination leads to a "person's valuing himself or herself above other people and above other living things." By contrast, "Social-Altruistic" factors reorient a person's priorities more broadly, to include the "costs to or benefits for other people, be they individuals, a neighborhood, a social network, a country, or all humanity." And, taking it further still, a "Biospheric" orientation elevates the importance of all living things, placing the concerns of animals and nature more generally on par with human considerations.

Reflecting on this framework, P. Wesley Schultz asserts that "environmental concern is tied to a person's notion of self and the degree to which people define themselves as independent, interdependent with other people, or interdependent with all living things."[9] Cynthia McPherson Frantz and F. Stephan Mayer extend this claim further, arguing that a sense of interdependence with others and the world is "one of the few psychological forces strong enough to compete with the prevailing counterforces required to engage in environmentally responsible behavior."[10]

Pilgrimage consistently immerses us in a natural context, and often a wonderfully glorious one at that. Nolan and Nolan have studied this relationship in Europe and determined that 48% of major pilgrimage sites have striking natural features (like caves, water, and trees).[11] This has lasting ramifications from an environmental perspective. As Frantz and Mayer have proven empirically, those who score higher on their "Connectedness to Nature" scale consistently demonstrate greater levels of environmentally responsible behavior. Furthermore, pilgrimage also shifts our priorities from ourselves to others, by promoting a "small-self effect" and exposing us to *communitas*. Combined, these twin influences are likely to diminish the prominence of the "Egoistic" factor, while elevating the importance of "Social-Altruistic" and "Biospheric" considerations.

Seb Yaño, however, saw an even more direct role for pilgrimage to play in the climate struggle. His mission to save the world originated from a deeply personal loss: his father's hometown, Tacloban, perched above San Pablo Bay in the Philippines, was ravaged by Typhoon Haiyan in 2013.[12] While Yaño already served as a climate change negotiator for the Philippines at that point, he soon left his government role in order to meet the growing threat with greater urgency and fewer restrictions.

In 2015, he launched The People's Pilgrimage, a 930-mile journey from the Vatican to Paris, designed to deliver him in the French city just in time for a UN climate meeting. Leaving Rome, following a blessing from Pope Francis, Saño declared, "By walking together, we will show climate change as the great challenge of our time—and that it can be overcome."[13] Upon arrival in Paris, Saño and his fellow pilgrims assembled a collection of shoes from around the world, to represent the diverse people, all around the globe, who were already being affected by climate change. This included a pair from the pope.

Three years later, Saño hit the road again, this time on The Climate Pilgrimage. As before, he departed the Vatican for a UN climate conference, though this time the destination was Katowice, Poland. He was joined on this occasion by a group of fellow Filipino pilgrims—survivors of the typhoon in Tacloban—and others from around the world. The journey was marked by an overwhelming display of community and connection, as local hosts saw to their every need, while opportunities abounded for discussions with other climate activists on how to effect change. Even after arriving in Poland, their journey continues.[14]

This is no mere intellectual exercise. Pilgrimage traditions are at risk, like everything else, as a consequence of climate change. A 2019 study by MIT and Loyola Marymount researchers found that the hajj, in particular, is at great risk of being made impractical when future pilgrimage seasons land during summer months.[15] Indeed, significant harm has likely already been done—the deadliest stampedes occurring during the hajj in recent memory have taken place during periods of surging heat and humidity. Meanwhile, forest fires have become a growing hazard in Spain and Portugal—along with many, many other places—and accompanying heat waves pose health risks for pilgrims on the Camino de Santiago.

If pilgrimage—and pilgrims—cannot contribute to the solution, it, too, stands to become a casualty of these surging calamities.

*   *   *   *   *

But this is supposed to be a conclusion—and ideally an uplifting one! In my experience, though, the conclusion of pilgrimage is always imbued with melancholy sentiments. It's not just the challenge of re-entry, which I discussed in the introduction; it's also the loss of something wonderful, something profound.

Perhaps, though, in the same way that a failure of imagination blinded me to the broader potential of pilgrimage, there's a conceptual failure at work here—a fundamental misunderstanding of when and where pilgrimages begin and end. In *Returning from Camino*, Alexander John Shaia exhorts walking pilgrims on the Camino de Santiago to reconsider the language we use—to not think of Santiago de Compostela as the destination, but rather as the "turn around point."[16] The pilgrimage, in his view, continues long after we return home.

There's a risk, Alexander told me, that pilgrimage "can be like an elixir and then we come back home and crash and think it was all just a dream about some other place and some other person." For all too many, this proves true. Instead of spurring transformative change, our pilgrimage experience can loom over our re-entry like a haunting reminder of untapped potential.

The issue, as Alexander explained it, is that "you don't fully change on the Camino. What happens on the Camino is you become awake to what you want to do differently. You might begin to make those changes when you are in that environment," but unfortunately, once back in your "ordinary everyday world," it's easy to go astray. You have to prepare diligently to carry the work forward. "I don't want to say that the Camino is not transformative," Alexander added, "but it tills the soil and awakens us and presents us with questions and issues to face, but then we have to go home, and we have to actually make those part of our everyday reality."[17]

Such is the possibility and peril of pilgrimage: any foray into a liminal space liberates us from the "tyranny of the now" but it comes with a firm expiration date. It will end. We will return to our "normal" lives.

There are no money-back guarantees here. Pilgrimage isn't a miracle drug. Whether the target is personal growth or solving climate change, the journey is long and littered with pitfalls. But if you look closely, you can see the waymarks, and if you can endure the many setbacks along the way, the road will lead you ever onward.

*   *   *   *   *

After my first pilgrimage on the Camino de Santiago, I knew with total clarity that I would return with students. This would become a focal point of my career. Indeed, thanks to the steadfast support of a former teacher, I was back in Spain within two years, leading my first group of high schoolers before I had even been hired into my first full-time teaching position. I marveled then and I marvel now that nine families had decided to trust their children into my inexperienced care. I talk a good game.

The honeymoon was over after three days. I dragged a group of dead-on-their-feet students around Pamplona to deliver the curriculum I had prepped and was damn sure I was going to deliver. Blisters and sore feet had already sapped many in the group of their good cheer. My loyal co-leader looked me square in the face and said he couldn't continue in this way.

I had planned out every inch of this trip. These challenges were an indictment of my judgment and a reminder of my glaring inexperience. I buried my face in my albergue pillow that night and wept (apologies to whoever got it the next night). I struggled to focus on viable adjustments we could make, however nightmare scenarios incessantly butted in, forcing me to reckon with the possibility of an interrupted pilgrimage, an early trip home, a personal and professional failure.

"I firmly believe now," Phil Cousineau told me years later, "if there isn't a dark night of the soul, if there isn't a descent into despair, into doubt, it's not a pilgrimage."[18] Unfortunately, I didn't know that then!

In the days that followed, we made some modest changes. For starters, we slept in later the next morning—at least, those who were able to sleep did! Beyond that, I scrapped many of my planned mini-lessons. They had value, but they were also exercises in ego, consistently placing myself at the center of attention. Instead, the students' journey needed to be the heart of the experience.

At the same time, though, I rejected more dramatic modifications. In hindsight, strange as it sounds, it's one of the braver moments of my life. The obvious answer was to change the itinerary, shorten the daily stages, come to terms with skipping ahead a bit by bus or train to ease the strain. When things go wrong, that kind of decisive action seems like the hallmark of responsive leadership. And yet, I fervently believed in the schedule that I had prepared. I had faith that we could endure these early setbacks, that we urgently *needed* these setbacks. They would test us, but they would also galvanize us.

When is trusting to faith a noble act and when is it incorrigible stubbornness? When is it both?

Regardless, the faith was rewarded. We settled into a routine, we came together as a group, and we walked with ever growing confidence and joy. We arrived in Santiago de Compostela early on a summer morning, filled with awe and pride, and a day later continued on to Finisterre. On our last night of pilgrimage, we sat on the rocky promontory, more deeply connected than any group I had ever been part of, watching the sun set and reflecting on how much we had overcome. What I remember most, though, is the walk back. The lighthouse at the world's end sits several kilometers outside of town, so those returning after sunset face a long stroll along a dark road. Far from tired, the students in my group raced ahead towards the promise of late-night burgers, while my co-leaders and I took up the rear. My mentor and friend Jon turned to me about mid-way and said, "you've created something special." And then he asked, "So... Rome next summer?"

We went to Rome the next summer. Where will you go?

APPENDIX

By Lauren Selden, Catie Kean, and Dave Whitson

Short descriptions of the pilgrimages spotlighted in this text follow. These are intended to provide context while reading and then to also offer a starting point, should you be interested in exploring them further. It should go without saying that concise summaries cannot hope to capture the richness of these sacred destinations and some glaring omissions may occur as a consequence of their brevity. Apologies in advance!

Abraham Path (Middle East)

This still-developing pilgrimage route follows the journey made by Abraham and his family 4000 years ago. William Ury founded the project in 2004 and believed that the shared narrative of Abraham as the forefather of Judaism, Islam, and Christianity could provide unity in a region fraught with turmoil. The path starts in Harran (modern day Turkey) where Abraham's journey began and ends in Hebron (the West Bank) where he is thought to be buried. Currently, roughly 1,500 kilometers of trails have been laid out through Turkey, Iraq, Jordan, Israel, Palestine, Jordan, KSA, and Egypt. **Getting Started:** abrahampath.org

Banaras (India)

One of India's most sacred pilgrimage sites, Banaras (also known as Avimukta, Varanasi, and Kashi) is believed to be the greatest shrine on the Ganges River and a destination particularly revered among those near the ends of their lives. Hindus hold that those who die and are cremated in

Banaras, with their ashes released into the Ganges, are liberated from the reincarnation cycle. A 50-mile sacred path surrounds Banaras—the Panchakroshi Parikrama—and pilgrims who complete the five-day journey visit 108 temples along their way. **Getting Started:** Diana Eck's *Banaras: City of Light*

California Mission Trail (USA)

Known historically as El Camino Real ("The Royal Road"), the CMT is an 800-mile trail that spans roughly two-thirds of the length of California, from San Diego to Sonoma, though the original route extended south all the way to Loreto, Mexico. The trail connects the Jesuit and Franciscan missions established by Father Junípero Serra and others during the 18th and 19th centuries; its name honors the Spanish royalty that financed their work. Today, the route roughly parallels Highway 101. **Getting Started:** Sandy Brown's *Hiking and Cycling the California Missions Trail* and missionwalk.org

Camino de Santiago (Spain / Europe)

The Camino is a Catholic pilgrimage route that dates to the early 9th century, when the hermit Pelayo rediscovered the apostle St. James the Great's relics, which had been buried there following the miraculous transfer of those relics to Iberia after James's martyrdom. Pilgrims historically departed from their homes all over Europe, so the Camino is actually a network of pilgrim roads that converge upon Santiago de Compostela; many of these have been recovered now, spiderwebbing all across Western Europe and beyond. The most popular branch is the Camino Francés, linking Saint-Jean-Pied-de-Port, France with Santiago and drawing more than two hundred thousand pilgrims annually. Today's pilgrims come from all faith backgrounds and while most walk, others ride bikes and horses. **Getting Started:** National organizations operate in most English-speaking countries, including the US-based American Pilgrims on the Camino (americanpilgrims.org) and the UK-based Confraternity of St. James (csj.org.uk)

Canindé (Brazil)

A shrine venerating Saint Francis that draws pilgrims from throughout this rugged, rural part of Brazil—especially in October, during the Feast of Saint Francis—to worship in the Casa dos Milagres ("House of Miracles"). Most of these pilgrims journey—mostly by motorized vehicle—to Canindé in order to fulfil a promessa ("promise") made to St. Francis in exchange for intercessional healing. They come bearing ex-voto sculptures that symbolically represent parts of their bodies that benefited from this miraculous intervention. **Getting Started:** festa.santuariodecaninde.com

Golden Temple (Amritsar, India)

Also known as the Sri Harmandir Sahib, this is Sikhism's holiest temple, situated on the site of a former lake where the Buddha is believed to have meditated. Purifying waters, in which pilgrims bathe, surround the temple complex, while the kitchen serves free meals to more than 20,000 visitors daily—a hallmark of Sikh temples. **Getting Started:** sgpc.net

The Hajj (Saudi Arabia)

Obligatory for all Muslims, provided it is physically and financially viable, the hajj includes multiple elements but centers on the Kaaba in the sacred city of Mecca. Pilgrims generally travel in groups to Mecca during the last month of the Islamic calendar, though a "lesser" pilgrimage can occur year-round. While the hajj—and its carefully structured sequence of rituals—connects back to the life of Muhammed, beliefs hold that it is rooted even more deeply in the past, to Abraham's era. This pilgrimage is open exclusively to Muslims. **Virtual Tour:** interactive.aljazeera.com/aje/hajj360/index.html

Khembalung (Nepal)

This sacred place is a beyul, or "hidden valley" in the Himalayas, situated in a cave at 7200' above sea level. Tibetan Buddhists believe that the various beyul will become their refuges when evil overcomes humanity. Two trails lead to Khembalung: a difficult one for sinners, who fall from it into a lake, and an easy one for non-sinners. Buddhists hike to this extremely remote cave in order to meditate, worship, light lamps, make offerings, and ask that their wishes be fulfilled. **Getting Started:** Johan Reinhard's *Khembalung: The Hidden Valley*

Kumbh Mela (India)

This Hindu festival is the world's largest gathering of pilgrims; in 2019, it drew 50 million people in a single day. While currently associated with an eighth-century Hindu saint, Adi Shankara, it's more likely based on an older Hindu festival, Magha Mela. It attracts pilgrims to four sites, each on different rivers, in a twelve-year cycle. Each festival focuses on the pilgrim ritual of entering the river waters to wash away sins, but also includes fairs and entertainment, among other traditions. **Getting Started:** kumbhmela.com

Lough Derg (Ireland)

St. Patrick's Purgatory is an ancient place of pilgrimage on Station Island in Lough Derg, Ireland. Legend holds that God revealed a small cave on Station Island, called Purgatory, to St. Patrick during his life spent bringing Catholicism to Ireland in the fifth century. Lough Derg has been a place of Catholic pilgrimage ever since. In the Middle Ages, pilgrims would fast for two weeks and then be locked, alone, in the cave for 24 hours. While some died, those who survived were believed to be absolved of the time in purgatory waiting for them after death. The cave has been closed since 1632, but many modern pilgrims still travel to Lough Derg, undergoing an intense three-day regimen of prayer and fasting that ends with a 24-hour vigil. **Getting Started:** loughderg.org

Lourdes (France)

This Catholic shrine in southeastern France attracts six million hopeful visitors each year. In 1858, the Blessed Virgin appeared to 14-year-old Bernadette Soubirous 18 times in a grotto just outside the village of Lourdes. She helped Bernadette find a spring in the grotto and asked that a chapel be built there. Pilgrims have flooded to Lourdes ever since in order to pray to Mary and St. Bernadette, as well as to bathe in the water from the spring in hope of miraculous cures for illnesses. Over 7000 unexplained cures have occurred at Lourdes since the 1858 apparitions; the sanctuary's medical bureau has affirmed that 70 of those cases qualify as miracles. **Getting Started:** lourdes-france.org/en

Pandharpur Wari (India)

This Hindu pilgrimage destination is the seat of Vithoba, a manifestation of Vishnu, in the state of Maharashtra. Pilgrims to Pandharpur converge from multiple points of departure, typically walking in support of a palanquin carrying the "paduka" (footprints) of Vithoba and local saints. Most walking pilgrimages take roughly three weeks. Upon arrival in Pandharpur, pilgrims visit the Vithoba Temple and bathe in the sacred waters of the Chandrabhaga River. A particular manifestation of this pilgrimage, Ashadi Ekadashi Wari, happens annually in the Hindu month of Ashadha and follows the exact same walking stages and schedule every year—one of the largest and oldest such traditions in human history. **Getting Started:** Deepak Phadnis's *Pandharpur Wari – A Walking Pilgrimage to Pandharpur*

Rocamadour (France)

Legend has it that St. Amadour (also believed to be the biblical tax-collector Zaccheus), after meeting Jesus, converting, and preaching the gospel for the rest of his life, founded a chapel dedicated to the Virgin Mary where the present-day village of Rocamadour, France, now sits. Pilgrims have visited Rocamadour to venerate the relics of St. Amadour and the statue of the Black Madonna, reputed to be carved by St. Amadour, since the 12th century, when the first miracle attributed to the image occurred there. Modern pilgrimage to Rocamadour is mostly by car or bus, but some walking pilgrims deviate slightly from the Via Podiensis, one of the Camino variants through France, in order to visit. **Getting Started:** vallee-dordogne.com/rocamadour

Run for the Wall (USA)

Run for the Wall is a motorcycle pilgrimage from Ontario, California, to the Vietnam Veterans Memorial in Washington, D.C. Started in 1989 by two Vietnam veterans, Run for the Wall gives veterans of all wars, as well as family members, friends, and active military personnel a chance to heal along their journey and to remember and honor those killed, wounded, and missing in action. The Run for the Wall organization also educates young people about wartime accountability and the importance of leaving no man behind. **Getting Started:** rftw.us

Saint Olav Ways (Norway)

The Saint Olav Ways are eight paths that lead through Scandinavia to the Nidaros Cathedral in Trondheim, Norway. The cathedral sits on top of the burial site of King Olav II, the patron saint of Norway, and has been a place of pilgrimage (in fact, the most important place of pilgrimage in Norway) since his canonization in 1031. The most popular of the Saint Olav Ways is the Gudbrandsdalen path, which starts in Norway's capital, Oslo. **Getting Started**: pilegrimsleden.no/en

Santuario de Chimayó (USA)

Roughly 300,000 pilgrims travel to this shrine in New Mexico each year, focused primarily on Holy Week. Some travel by motorized vehicle, but others walk from different parts of the state, often in groups. Chimayó includes two important chapels. First, the Lord of Esquipulas Chapel contains "el pocito," or the small hole in the floor providing access to "holy dirt" that is associated with miracle cures. While pilgrims traditionally ate the dirt, today's visitors opt to rub the dirt onto their skin, or simply take it with them. The second site, Santo Niño de Atocha, commemorates an Easter pilgrimage made by US soldiers who prayed to Santo Niño while enduring the Bataan Death March and lived to express their gratitude. **Getting Started:** holychimayo.us

Santuario de Guadalupe (Mexico)

Already a sacred site among Aztecs prior to colonization, in time Guadalupe became the most significant Catholic shrine in North America. The story goes that a baptized young Aztec was tasked by an apparition with building a church in service to the Virgin Mary. Through his persistence—and a bit of miraculous help from Mary—he ultimately persuaded the archbishop to carry this out, with the first shrine finished on Tepeyac Hill in 1660. The first basilica followed in 1695, and then a second basilica was added next door in 1976. Attendance at the shrine peaks on December 12, the Virgin of Guadalupe's annual feast day, when perhaps nine million worshippers pay homage, some walking from quite a distance. **Getting Started:** virgendeguadalupe.org.mx/en/

Shikoku's 88 Temples (Japan)

This Buddhist pilgrimage around Shikoku follows in the footsteps of Kōbō Daishi, who spent his life on this island in the 8th and 9th centuries. Priest, poet, and imperial advisor during his life, he was elevated to sainthood afterward, and remains revered across Japan today. Shikoku's 88 temples all stay within relatively close proximity to the coast, thus making the pilgrimage essentially a circumambulation of the island, spanning anywhere between 1100 and 1400km. Walking pilgrims, though, are a relative minority, as many of Shikoku's pilgrims travel by bus. **Getting Started:** shikokuhenrotrail.com

Sri Pada (Sri Lanka)

Also known as Adam's Peak, the Holy Footprint, and Samanala Kanda, this mountain is the most sacred pilgrimage site in Sri Lanka, revered by Hindus, Buddhists, Muslims, and Christians alike. Buddhists discovered the "footprint" first, as far back as 3rd century BC, and attributed it to the Buddha on his last visit to Sri Lanka. Portuguese Christians, meanwhile, asserted in the 16th century that it belonged to Saint Thomas. Finally, Arab travelers linked it to Adam himself, arguing that this was where the poor fellow spent a thousand years serving penance on one foot. "Pilgrimage season" on the mountain runs from December to May, hitting its peak in January and February, with up to 20,000 people making the climb on weekends during those months. **Getting Started:** sripada.org

Via Francigena (Italy, Switzerland, France, England)

Forget "all roads lead to Rome;" *this* is the most fully recovered medieval pilgrim road to Rome in existence today, leading from Canterbury, England to Saint Peter's Square in the Vatican. In the Middle Ages it also continued to Apulia, where pilgrims could catch ships to travel to the Holy Land; that route through Italy has been recently recovered as well and is known as the Via Francigena Sud. The primary medieval itinerary for this route comes from Sigeric the Serious, Archbishop of Canterbury, who walked to Rome and back to England in the 10th century and documented his journey for posterity. While its recovery has not been marked by the same dramatic resurgence of walking pilgrims as Spain's Camino, it now draws a consistent stream, especially from Tuscany onward. **Getting Started:** viefrancigene.org/en

Walsingham (England)

This village in Southeastern England has drawn pilgrims since 1061, when the Virgin Mary appeared to a Walsingham noblewoman three times, telling her to build a replica of the House of the Holy Family. That replica then assembled itself miraculously when the noblewoman provided the proper materials. A priory was built around it about a century later. Walsingham functioned as a significant pilgrimage destination from that time until King Henry VIII destroyed the priory during the English Reformation. Pilgrimage to Walsingham has undergone a revival over the last 120 years. Modern Walsingham pilgrimage consists of visiting the 14th century Slipper Chapel, removing shoes, and then walking the final mile barefoot from there to the Shrine of Our Lady of Walsingham. The shrine contains copies of the Holy House and the venerated image of Mary that were destroyed in the 16th century. **Getting Started:** walsinghamanglican.org.uk

Wutai Shan (China)

One of China's four major Buddhist mountains, Mount Wutai actually includes five main peaks, ranging from 2,485 to 3,061 meters of elevation. The first temple was built here more than 2,000 years ago and at its peak some 360 temples were in operation. While only 68 survive today, they are joined by 53 Buddhist monasteries along with tens of thousands of Buddha statues. **Getting Started:** whc.unesco.org/en/list/1279

BIBLIOGRAPHY

Introduction

[1] Alan Morinis, *Sacred Journeys: The Anthropology of Pilgrimage* (Greenwood, NY: Greenwood Press, 1992).
[2] Luigi Tomasi, "Homo Viator. From Pilgrimage to Religious Tourism via the Journey" in: *From Medieval Pilgrimage to Religious Tourism*, ed. William H. Swatos, Jr & Luigi Tomasi, *The Social and Cultural Economics of Piety* (Westport: Praeger, 2002).
[3] Richard Barber, *Pilgrimages* (Woodbridge: Boydell & Brewer, 1993).
[4] Victor Turner and Edith Turner, *Image and Pilgrimage in Christian Culture* (New York: Columbia University Press, 1978).

Opening the Door

[1] Einar Lunga, "Den Terapeutiske Veien," *Pilegrimen*, 2, 10 (2006), 47–51; Nanna Natalia Karpinska Dam Jorgensen, *El Camino de Santiago: Walking Oneself to Wellbeing, Reclaiming and Reinforcing One's Spirit*, Norwegian University of Science and Technology: MPhil dissertation, 2008.
[2] WHO, "Physical Inactivity: A Global Public Health Problem," *World Health Organization*, https://www.who.int/dietphysicalactivity/factsheet_inactivity/en
[3] Denise Mitten, Jillisa R. Overholt, Francis I. Haynes, Chiara C. D'Amore, and Janet C. Ady, "Hiking: A Low-Cost, Accessible Intervention to Promote Health Benefits," *American Journal of Lifestyle Medicine* 12, 4 (2018): 302–10.
[4] Mayo Foundation for Medical Education and Research, "What are the risks of sitting too much? – Answers from James A. Levine, M.D., Ph.D.," https://www.mayoclinic.org/hea lthy-lifestyle/adult-health/expert-answers/sitting/faq-20058005.
[5] Leandro Fornias Machado de Rezende, Maurício Rodrigues Lopes, Juan Pablo Rey-López, Victor Keihan Rodrigues Matsudo, Olinda do Carmo Luiz, "Sedentary Behavior and Health Outcomes: An Overview of Systematic Reviews," *PLOS ONE*, 9, 8 (2014). doi: 10.1371/journal.pone.0105620
[6] SC Gilchrist, VJ Howard, T Akinyemiju, et al., "Association of Sedentary Behavior with Cancer Mortality in Middle-aged and Older US Adults," *JAMA Oncol,* published online June 18, 2020. doi:10.1001/jamaoncol.2020.2045
[7] University of Texas M. D. Anderson Cancer Center, "Sedentary behavior independently predicts cancer mortality: Replacing sitting time with 30 minutes of activity associated with lower risk of cancer death," *ScienceDaily*, www.sciencedaily.com/releases/2020/06/200618150311.htm.

[8] WHO, "Obesity and Overweight," *World Health Organization,* https://www.who.int/news-room/fact-sheets/detail/obesity-and-overweight

[9] Penny Gordon-Larsen, Ningqi Hou, Steve Sidney, Barbara Sternfeld, Cora E Lewis, David R Jacobs Jr, and Barry M Popkin, "Fifteen-year longitudinal trends in walking patterns and their impact on weight change," *American Journal of Clinical Nutrition,* 89 (2010), 19-26.

[10] Yannick Stephan, Angelina R. Sutin, Martina Luchetti, Grégoire Bosselut, Antonio Terracciano, "Physical activity and personality development over twenty years: Evidence from three longitudinal samples," *Journal of Research in Personality,* 73 (2018), 173-179.

[11] Neil Klepeis, William Nelson, Wayne Ott, et al., "The National Human Activity Pattern Survey (NHAPS): a resource for assessing exposure to environmental pollutants," *Journal of Exposure Science & Environmental Epidemiology,* 11 (2001), 231–252.

[12] European Commission, "Indoor air pollution: new EU research reveals higher risks than previously thought," *European Commission,* https://ec.europa.eu/commission/presscorner/detail/en/IP_03_1278

[13] Edie Littlefield Sundby, TheMission Walker (Nashville: Harper Collins, 2017).

[14] Qing Li, *Forest Bathing: How Trees Can Help You Find Health and Happiness* (New York: Viking, 2018).

[15] Nancy Louise Frey, *Pilgrim Stories: On and Off the Road to Santiago* (Berkeley: University of California Press, 1998).

[16] Lee Hoinacki, *El Camino: Walking to Santiago de Compostela* (University Park: Penn State UP, 1996).

[17] Roger Ulrich, "View through a Window May Influence Recovery from Surgery," *Science,* 224, 4647 (1984), 420-421.

[18] Seong-Hyun Park and Richard Mattson, "Ornamental indoor plants in hospital rooms enhanced health outcomes of patients recovering from surgery," *Journal of Alternative and Complementary Medicine,* 15, 9 (2009), 975-80.

[19] Mathew P. White, Sabine Pahl, Katherine Ashbullby, Stephen Herbert, and Michael H. Depledge, "Feelings of restoration from recent nature visits," *Journal of Environmental Psychology,* 35 (2013), 40-51.

[20] Ian Alcock, MP White, BW Wheeler, LE Fleming, and MH Depledge, "Longitudinal effects on mental health of moving to greener and less green urban areas," *Environmental Science and Technology,* 48, 2 (2014), 1247-1255.

[21] Jia Wei Zhang, Paul K. Piff, Ravi Iyer, Spassena Koleva, Dacher Keltner, "An occasion for unselfing: Beautiful nature leads to prosociality," *Journal of Environmental Psychology,* 37 (2014), 61-72.

[22] George MacKerron and Susana Mourato, "Happiness is greater in natural environments," *Global Environmental Change,* 23, 5 (2013), 992-1000.

[23] Diane Eck, *Banaras: City of Light* (New York: Columbia UP, 1999).

[24] Roger Housden, *Sacred Journeys in a Modern World* (New York: Simon & Schuster, 1998).

[25] Ann Grodzins Gold, *Fruitful Journeys: The Ways of Rajasthani Pilgrims* (Long Grove: Waveland Press, 2000).

[26] E.Valentine Daniel, *Fluid Signs: Being a Person the Tamil Way* (Berkeley: University of California Press, 1984).

[27] Surinder Mohan Bhardwaj, *Hindu Places of Pilgrimage in India* (Berkeley: University of California Press, 1983).

[28] Rosemary Mahoney, *The Singular Pilgrim: Travels on Sacred Ground* (Boston: Houghton Mifflin, 2003).

[29] I-Min Lee & David Buchner, "The Importance of Walking to Public Health," *Medicine & Science in Sports & Exercise*, 40, 7 (2008), S512-S518.

[30] Gordon-Larsen et al, "Fifteen-year longitudinal trends in walking patterns and their impact on
weight change."

[31] Carl Caspersen & Janet Fulton, "Epidemiology of Walking and Type 2 Diabetes," *Medicine & Science in Sports & Exercise*, 40, 7 (2008), S519-S528.

[32] Lee & Buchner, "The Importance of Walking to Public Health."

[33] Regan Howard, Michael Leitzmann, Martha Linet, and D. Michal Freedman, "Physical Activity and Breast Cancer Risk among Pre- and Postmenopausal Women in the U.S. Radiologic Technologists Cohort." *Cancer Causes & Control*, 20, 3 (2009), 323-33.

[34] Frank Hu, Meir Stampfer, Graham Colditz, et al., "Physical Activity and Risk of Stroke in Women," *JAMA*, 283, 22 (2000), 2961–2967.

[35] American Geriatrics Society, "Guideline for the prevention of falls in older persons," *Journal of the American Geriatrics Society*, 49, 5 (2001).

[36] Dave Whitson, "Episode 47 – Into the Thin," The Camino Podcast, July 13, 2020, https://soundcloud.com/user-939742370/episode-47-into-the-thin

[37] Stephen Drew, *Into the Thin: A Pilgrimage Walk Across Northern Spain* (Pawcatuck: Homebound Publications, 2020).

[38] Shane O'Mara, *In Praise of Walking: A New Scientific Explanation* (New York: Norton, 2020).

[39] Sophie E. Carter, Richard Draijer, Sophie M. Holder, Louise Brown, Dick H. J. Thijssen, and Nicola D. Hopkins, "Regular walking breaks prevent the decline in cerebral blood flow associated with prolonged sitting," *Journal of Applied Psychology*, 125, 3 (2018), 790-798.

[40] Marily Oppezzo and Daniel Schwartz, "Give Your Ideas Some Legs: The Positive Effect of Walking on Creative Thinking," *Journal of Experimental Psychology*, 40, 4 (2014), 1142-1152.

[41] Kristine Yaffe, Deborah Barnes, Michael Nevitt, Li-Yung Lui, Kenneth Covinsky, "A Prospective Study of Physical Activity and Cognitive Decline in Elderly Women," *JAMA Internal Medicine*, 161 (2001), 1703-1708.

[42] Eck, *Banaras*.

[43] Housden, *Sacred Journeys in a Modern World*.

[44] Nanna Natalia Karpinska Dam Jorgensen, *El Camino Santiago: Walking oneself to wellbeing, reclaiming and reinforcing one's spirit*, NTNU, 2008.

[45] James Blumenthal and Lephuong Ong, "A commentary on 'Exercise and Depression': And the Verdict Is…." *Mental Health and Physical Activity*, 2, 2 (2009), 97-99.

[46] Gregory Simon, "Should Psychiatrists Write the Exercise Prescription for Depression?," *American Journal of Psychiatry*, 175, 1 (2018).

[47] Samuel B. Harvey, Ph.D., Simon Øverland, Stephani L. Hatch, et al, "Exercise and the Prevention of Depression: Results of the HUNT Cohort Study," *American Journal of Psychiatry*, 175, 1 (2018), 28-36.

[48] Jason Duvall, "Enhancing the benefits of outdoor walking with cognitive engagement strategies," *Journal of Environmental Psychology*, 31 (2011), 27-35.

[49] Stephanie Revell & John McLeod, "Experiences of therapists who integrate walk and talk into their professional practice," *Counseling and Psychotherapy Research*, 16, 1 (2016).

[50] Denice Clark, *Adult Clients' Experience of Walk-and-Talk Therapy*, Walden University, 2019.

[51] Marcus Johansson, Terry Hartig, Henk Staats, "Psychological Benefits of Walking: Moderation by
Company and Outdoor Environment," *Applied Psychology*, 3, 3 (2001), 261-280.

[52] Jo Thompson Coon, K. Boddy, K. Stein, et al, "Does Participating in Physical Activity in Outdoor Natural
Environments Have a Greater Effect on Physical and Mental Wellbeing than Physical Activity Indoors? A Systematic Review," *Environmental Science & Technology*, 45 (2011), 1761-1772.

[53] Jules Pretty, Jo Peacock, Martin Sellens, & Murray Griffin, "The mental and physical health outcomes of green exercise," *International Journal of Environmental Health Research*, 15, 5 (2005), 319-337.

[54] Marc G. Berman, Ethan Kross, Katherine Krpan, et al, "Interacting with nature improves cognition and affect for individuals with depression," *Journal of Affective Disorders*, 140 (2012), 300-305.

[55] Sean Slavin, "Walking as Spiritual Practice: The Pilgrimage to Santiago de Compostela," *Body & Society*, 9, 3 (2003), 1-18.

[56] Sarah Hanson & Andy Jones, "Is there evidence that walking groups have health benefits?," *Journal of Sports Medicine*, 49 (2015), 710-715.

[57] Lydia Kwak, Stef Kremers, Anthony Walsh, & Hans Brug, "How is your walking group running?," *Health Education*, 106 (2006), 21-31.

[58] John M. Stanley, "The great Maharashtrian pilgrimage : Pandharpur and Alandi," in *Sacred Journeys: The Anthropology of Pilgrimage,* ed. Alan Morinis (Greenwood, NY: Greenwood Press, 1992).

[59] Simon Coleman, "Putting it All Together Again: Healing and Incarnation in Walsingham," in *Pilgrimage and
Healing,* eds. Jill Dubisch and Michael Winkelman (Tucson University of Arizona Press, 2005).

[60] Tatjana Schnell and Sarah Pali, "Pilgrimage today: the meaning-making potential of ritual," *Mental Health, Religion & Culture*, 16, 9 (2013), 887-902.

[61] Anna Davidsson Bremborg, "Creating sacred space by walking in silence: Pilgrimage in a late modern Lutheran context," *Social Compass*, 60, 4 (2013), 544-560.

[62] Michelle N. Shiota , Dacher Keltner & Amanda Mossman, "The nature of awe: Elicitors, appraisals, and effects
on self-concept," *Cognition and Emotion*, 21, 5 (2007), 944-963.

[63] Alain de Botton, *How to Travel* (The School of Life Press, 2019).

[64] Craig L. Anderson, Maria Monroy, and Dacher Keltner, "Awe in Nature Heals: Evidence From Military Veterans, At-Risk Youth and College Students," *Emotion*, 18, 8 (2018), 1195-1202.

[65] Eric Weiner, "Where Heaven and Earth Come Closer," *New York Times,* March 9, 2012, https://www.nytimes.com/2012/03/11/travel/thin-places-where-we-are-jolted-out-of-old-ways-of-seeing-the-world.html

[66] Ann Armbrecht, *Thin Places: A Pilgrimage Home* (New York: Columbia University Press, 2009).

[67] Phil Cousineau, *The Art of Pilgrimage* (San Francisco: Conari Press, 1998).

[68] Eck, *Banaras*

[69] Johan Reinhard, "Khembalung: The Hidden Valley," *Kailash, A Journal of Himalayan Studies* (1978).

[70] Dave Whitson, "Episode 4 – Phil's Camino," The Camino Podcast, December 20, 2015, https://soundcloud.com/user-939742370/episode4-phils-camino

[71] Phil's Camino, directed by Jessica Lewis and Annie O'Neil (Los Angeles, CA: Everyday Camino, 2016).

[72] Avril Maddrell, "Moving and being moved: More-than-walking and talking on pilgrimage walks in the Manx landscape," *Culture and Religion*, 14, 1 (2013), 63-77.

[73] Eck, *Banaras.*

[74] Edit Littlefield Sundby, "The Coronavirus Threat Hasn't Stopped Me From Walking," *Wall Street Journal*, April 1, 2020, https://www.wsj.com/articles/the-coronavirus-threat-hasnt-stopped-me-from-walking-11585780196.

Looking Within

[1] Kym Wilson, *The Path You Make* (Self-Published, 2019).

[2] Beth Jusino, *Walking to the End of the World* (Seattle: Mountaineers Books, 2018).

[3] John Robinson, "Americans Less Rushed But No Happier: 1965–2010 Trends in Subjective Time and Happiness," *Social Indicators Research*, 113 (2013), 1091-1104, DOI 10.1007/s11205-012-0133-6.

[4] Daniel S. Hamermesh and Jungmin Lee, "Stressed Out on Four Continents: Time Crunch or Yuppie Kvetch?." *The Review of Economics and Statistics* 89, 2 (2007), 374-383.

[5] Jordan Etkin, Ioannis Evangelidis, and Jennifer Aaker, "Pressed for Time? Goal Conflict Shapes How Time Is Perceived, Spent, and Valued," *Journal of Marketing Research* 52, 3 (2015), 394–406. doi:10.1509/jmr.14.0130.

[6] Melanie Rudd, Kathleen Vohs, and Jennifer Aaker, "Awe Expands People's Perception of Time, Alters Decision Making, and Enhances Well-Being," *Psychological Science* 23, 10 (2012), 1130-1136. DOI: 10.1177/0956797612438731

[7] Dave Whitson, "Episode 31 – John & Rebekah," The Camino Podcast, November 22, 2019, https://soundcloud.com/user-939742370/episode-31-john-rebekah

[8] Gallup, *State of the Global Workplace* (New York: Gallup Press, 2017).

[9] Johann Hari, *Lost Connections: Why You're Depressed and How to Find Hope* (London: Bloomsbury, 2018).

[10] Brad Genereux, *A Soldier to Santiago* (Blackside, 2016).

[11] Dave Whitson, "Episode 32 – Veterans on the Camino," The Camino Podcast, November 30, 2019, https://soundcloud.com/user-939742370/episode-32-veterans-on-the-camino.

[12] WHO, "Depression," *World Health Organization*, https://www.who.int/news-room/fact-sheets/detail/depression.

[13] Kerri Smith, "Mental health: A world of depression," *Nature* 515, 7526 (2014).

[14] Roosa Tikkanen, Katharine Fields, Reginald D. Williams II, and Melinda K. Abrams, *Mental Health Conditions and Substance Use: Comparing U.S. Needs and Treatment Capacity with Those in Other High-Income Countries* (Commonwealth Fund, May 2020). https://doi.org/10.26099/09ht-rj07.

[15] A.H. Weinberger, M. Gbedemah, A. M. Martinez, D. Nash, S. Galea, and R. D. Goodwin, "Trends in depression prevalence in the USA from 2005 to 2015: widening disparities in vulnerable groups," *Psychological Medicine* 48 (2017), 1308-1315. https://doi.org/10.1017/S0033291717002781

[16] Timothy Egan, *Pilgrimage to Eternity: From Canterbury to Rome in Search of a Faith* (New York City: Viking, 2019).

[17] Zahra Vahedi and Alyssa Saiphoo, "The association between smartphone use, stress, and anxiety: A meta-analytic review," *Stress and Health* 34 (2018), 347-358. https://doi.org/10.1002/smi.2805

[18] Ric Steele, Jeffrey Hall, and Jennifer L. Christofferson, "Conceptualizing Digital Stress in Adolescents and Young Adults: Toward the Development of an Empirically Based Model," *Clinical Child and Family Psychology Review* 23 (2020), 15-26. https://doi.org/10.1007/s10567-019-00300-5

[19] Leonard Reinecke, Stefan Aufenanger, Manfred E. Beutel, et al, "Digital Stress over the Life Span," *Media Psychology* 0 (2016), 1-26. DOI: 10.1080/15213269.2015.1121832

[20] Holly B. Shakya and Nicholas A. Christakis, "Association of Facebook Use With Compromised Well-Being: A Longitudinal Study," *American Journal of Epidemiology* 185, 3 (2017), 203-211. DOI: 10.1093/aje/kww189

[21] Cal Newport, *Digital Minimalism* (New York: Portfolio/Penguin, 2019).

[22] Turner and Turner, *Image and Pilgrimage in Christian Culture*; Victor Turner, *Dramas, Fields, and Metaphors: Symbolic Action in Human Society* (Ithaca: Cornell University Press, 1974).

[23] Cousineau, *The Art of Pilgrimage*.

[24] Frey, *Pilgrim Stories*.

[25] Johnnie Walker, *It's About Time: A Call to the Camino de Santiago* (Hampshire: Redemptorist Publications, 2019).

[26] Dave Whitson, "Episode 27 – Johnnie Walker's Santiago," The Camino Podcast, November 5, 2016, https://soundcloud.com/user-939742370/episode27-johnnie-walkers-santiago.

[27] Francis Jauréguiberry, "La déconnexion aux technologies de communication," *Réseaux* 4, 186 (2014). 15-49. DOI 10.3917/res.186.0015

[28] Elizabeth Weiss Ozorak, "The View from the Edge: Pilgrimage and Transformation," in *On the Road to Being There: Studies in Pilgrimage and Tourism in Late Modernity*, ed. William H. Swatos, Jr. (Leiden: Brill, 2006).

[29] Ian Reader, *Making Pilgrimages: Meaning and Practice in Shikoku* (Honolulu: University of Hawaii Press, 2004).

[30] Andreas Nordin, "The Cognition of Hardship Experience in Himalayan Pilgrimage," *Numen* 58, 5/6 (2011), 632-673.

[31] Dubisch and Winkelman, *Pilgrimage and Healing*.

[32] G. William Farthing, *The Psychology of Consciousness* (Englewood Cliffs, N.J.: Prentice Hall, 1992).

[33] Jill Dubisch, "A Vietnam Veterans Motorcycle Pilgrimage," in *Pilgrimage and Healing*, eds. Jill Dubisch and Michael Winkelman (Tucson University of Arizona Press, 2005).

[34] Ginny Bartolone, "I Physically and Emotionally Broke Down on the Camino de Santiago, But Left with Less Anxiety and Depression," *Yahoo!*, https://www.yahoo.com/news/physically-emotionally-broke-down-camino-220000878.html

[35] Dave Whitson, host, "Episode 34 – How Strange It Will Be To Come Home," The Camino Podcast, December 8, 2019, https://soundcloud.com/user-939742370/episode-34-how-strange-it-will-be-to-come-home.

[36] Mihaly Csikszentmihalyi, *Flow: The Psychology of Optimal Experience* (New York: HarperCollins, 1991).

[37] Reader, *Making Pilgrimages*.

[38] Nanna Natalia Karpinska Dam Jorgensen, "The Processes, Effects and Therapeutics of Pilgrimage Walking the St. Olav Way," 2020, https://www.researchgate.net/publication/339238163

[39] Rudd et al, "Awe Expands People's Perception of Time, Alters Decision Making, and Enhances Well-Being,"

[40] Yang Bai, Laura A. Maruskin, Serena Chen, et al, "Awe, the Diminished Self, and Collective Engagement: Universals and Cultural Variations in the Small Self," *Journal of Personality and Social Psychology* 113, 2 (2017), 185-209. https://doi.org/10.1037/pspa0000087

[41] Libin Jiang, Jun Yin, Dongmei Mei, et al, "Awe Weakens the Desire for Money," *Journal of Pacific Rim Psychology* 12 (2018). DOI: 10.1017/prp.2017.27

[42] Alethea Koh, Eddie Tong, Alexander Yuen, "The buffering effect of awe on negative affect towards lost possessions," *Journal of Positive Psychology* 14, 2 (2019), 156-165. DOI: 10.1080/17439760.2017.1388431

[43] Whitson, "Episode 32 – Veterans on the Camino."

[44] Alexander John Shaia, *Returning from Camino* (Santa Fe: Quadratos, 2018).

[45] Leighanne Higgins and Kathy Hamilton, "Mini-miracles: Transformations of self from consumption of the Lourdes pilgrimage," *Journal of Business Research* 69 (2016), 25-32. https://doi.org/10.1016/j.jbusres.2015.07.017

[46] Sidney Greenfield and Antonio Mourão Cavalcante, "Pilgrimage Healing in Northeast Brazil: A Cultural-Biological Explanation," in *Pilgrimage and Healing*, eds. Dubisch & Winkelman.

[47] C. Lindsey King, "Pilgrimage, promises, and ex-votos : ingredients for healing in northeast Brazil," in *Pilgrimage and Healing*, eds. Dubisch & Winkelman.

[48] Jorgenson, "The Processes, Effects and Therapeutics of Pilgrimage Walking the St. Olav Way."

49 Heather Ann Warfield, *The Therapeutic Value of Pilgrimage: A Grounded Theory Study*, North Carolina State University, 2013.

Coming to the Table

1 Dave Whitson, host, "Episode 19: The Via Francigena," *The Camino Podcast*, June 12, 2016, https://soundcloud.com/user-939742370.
2 Dave Whitson, host, "Episode 43: The Winter Pilgrim & North American Pilgrimage," *The Camino Podcast*, June 29, 2020, https://soundcloud.com/user-939742370.
3 "Can people be trusted," *GSS Data Explorer*, accessed August 8, 2020, https://gssdataexplorer.norc.org/variables/441/vshow.
4 Esteban Ortiz-Ospina and Max Roser, "Trust," *Our World in Data*, 2016, https://ourworldindata.org/trust
5 OECD, *How's Life? 2015: Measuring Well-being* (Paris: OECD Publishing, 2015). https://doi.org/10.1787/how_life-2015-en.
6 Robert Putnam, *Bowling Alone: The Collapse and Revival of American Community* (New York City: Touchstone Books, 2001).
7 Robert Putnam, *The Upswing* (New York: Simon & Schuster, 2020).
8 Francesco Sarracino, "Social capital and subjective well-being trends: comparing 11 western European countries," *Journal of Socio-Economics* 39, no. 4 (2010): 482-517, doi: 10.1016/j.socec.2009.10.010; Francesco Sarracino and Malgorzata Mikucka, "Social capital in Europe from 1990 to 2012: trends, path-dependency and convergence," *Social Indicators Research* 131, no. 1 (2015): 407-432, doi: 10.1007/s11205-016-1255-z.
9 Esteban Ortiz-Ospina, "The rise of living alone: how one-person households are becoming increasingly common around the world," December 10, 2019, https://ourworldindata.org/living-alone.
10 Steve Watkins, *Pilgrim Strong: Rewriting my story on the Way of St. James* (Jonesboro, AK: self-published, 2017).
11 Dave Whitson, host, "Episode 44: How to Write a Pilgrimage Memoir," July 2, 2020, *The Camino Podcast*, https://soundcloud.com/user-939742370/episode-44-how-to-write-a-pilgrimage-memoir.
12 Johann Hari, *Lost Connections: Uncovering the Real Causes of Depression—and Unexpected Solutions* (New York City: Bloomsbury, 2018).
13 Ceylan Yeginsu, "U.K. Appoints a Minister for Loneliness," *The New York Times*, January 17, 2018, https://www.nytimes.com/2018/01/17/world/europe/uk-britain-loneliness.html.
14 Fay Bound Alberti, "This 'Modern Epidemic': Loneliness as an Emotion Cluster and a Neglected Subject in the History of Emotions," *Emotion Review* 10, no. 3 (2018): 242-254, doi: 10.1177/1754073918768876.
15 John T. Cacioppo and Stephanie Cacioppo, "Loneliness in the Modern Age: An Evolutionary Theory of Loneliness (ETL)," *Advances in Experimental Social Psychology* 58, no. 1 (2018): 127-197, doi: 10.1016/bs.aesp.2018.03.003.
16 Hari, *Lost Connections*.

[17] Victor Turner, *Dramas, Fields, and Metaphors: Symbolic Action in Human Society* (Ithaca, NY: Cornell University Press, 1974).

[18] Nancy Louise Frey, *Pilgrim Stories: On and Off the Road to Santiago* (Berkeley, CA: University of California Press, 1998).

[19] Chris Devereux and Elizabeth Carnegie, "Pilgrimage: Journeying Beyond Self," *Tourism Recreation Research* 31, no. 1 (2006): 47-56, doi: 10.1080/02508281.2006.11081246.

[20] Nanna Natalia Karpinska Dam Jorgensen, "Pilgrimage Walking as Green Prescription Self-therapy?" in *The Many Voices of Pilgrimage and Reconciliation*, eds. Ian S. McIntosh and Lesley D. Harman (Boston: CAB International, 2017), 124-137.

[21] Elizabeth Weiss Ozorak, "The View from the Edge: Pilgrimage and Transformation," in *On the Road to Being There: Studies in Pilgrimage and Tourism in Late Modernity*, ed. William H. Swatos, Jr. (Leiden: Brill, 2006).

[22] Avril Maddrell, "Moving and being moved: More-than-walking and talking on pilgrimage walks in the Manx landscape," *Culture and Religion* 14, no. 1 (2013): 63-77, doi: 10.1080/14755610.2012.756409.

[23] Paula Elizabeth Holmes-Rodman, "'They Told What Happened on the Road': Narrative and the Construction of Experiential Knowledge on the Pilgrimage to Chimayo, New Mexico," in *Intersecting Journeys: The Anthropology of Pilgrimage and Tourism*, eds. Ellen Badone and Sharon R. Roseman (Chicago: University of Illinois Press, 2004), 24-51.

[24] Shane O'Mara, *In Praise of Walking: A New Scientific Exploration* (New York City: W.W. Norton and Company, 2020).

[25] Anthony C. Gatrell, "Therapeutic mobilities: walking and 'steps' to wellbeing and health," *Health and Place* 22, no. 1 (2013): 98-106, 10.1016/j.healthplace.2013.04.002.

[26] Scott S. Wiltermuth and Chip Heath, "Synchrony and Cooperation," *Psychological Science* 20, no. 1 (2009): 1-5, doi: 10.1111/j.1467-9280.2008.02253x.

[27] Jesse Graham and Jonathan Haidt, "Beyond Beliefs: Religions Bind Individuals Into Moral Communities," *Personality and Social Psychology Review* 14, no. 1 (2010): 140-150, doi: 10.1177/1088868309353415.

[28] Ian Reader, *Making Pilgrimages: Meaning and Practice in Shikoku* (Honolulu: University of Hawaii Press, 2004).

[29] Shruti Tewari, Sammyh Khan, Nick Hopkins, Narayanan Srinivasan, Stephen Reicher, "Participation in Mass Gatherings Can Benefit Well-Being: Longitudinal and Control Data from a North Indian Hindu Pilgrimage Event," *PLoS One* 7, no. 10 (2012), doi: 10.1371/journal.pone.0047291.

[30] John Stanley, "The Great Maharashtrian Pilgrimage: Pandharpur and Alandi," in *Sacred Journeys: The Anthropology of Pilgrimage*," ed. Alan Morinis (Westport, CT: Greenwood Press, 1992), 65-88.

[31] Malcom X, Alex Haley, *The Autobiography of Malcolm X: As Told to Alex Haley* (New York: Ballantine, 1964).

[32] Rosemary Mahoney, *The Singular Pilgrim: Travels on Sacred Ground* (Boston: Houghton Mifflin, 2003).

[33] Jill Dubisch and Michael Winkelman, eds., *Pilgrimage and Healing* (Tucson, AZ: University of Arizona Press, 2014).

[34] Dave Whitson, host, "Episode 32: Veterans on the Camino," *The Camino Podcast*, November 30, 2019, https://soundcloud.com/user-939742370.

[35] Dave Whitson, host, "Episode 14: Walking with Family," *The Camino Podcast*, May 22, 2016, https://soundcloud.com/user-939742370.

[36] Whitson, "Episode 14: Walking with Family."

[37] Dave Whitson, host, "Episode 6: On the Primitive Way," *The Camino Podcast*, January 2, 2016, https://soundcloud.com/user-939742370.

[38] Cameron Powell, *Ordinary Magic: Promises I Kept to my Mother Through Life, Illness, and a Very Long Walk on the Camino de Santiago* (Herndon, VA: Mascot Books, 2018).

[39] Landon Roussel, *On the Primitive Way: Two Texan Brothers' Journey to Santiago de Compostela* (Halifax: Communitas Publishing, 2015).

[40] Kurt Koontz, *A Million Steps*, (Boise, ID: self-published, 2013).

Something Greater

[1] Abdellah Hammoudi, *A Season in Mecca: Narrative of a Pilgrimage* (New York City: Hill and Wang, 2006).

[2] Timothy Egan, *A Pilgrimage to Eternity: From Canterbury to Rome in Search of a Faith* (New York City: Viking, 2019).

[3] "In U.S., Decline of Christianity Continues at Rapid Pace," *Pew Research Center*, October 17, 2019, https://www.pewforum.org/2019/10/17/in-u-s-decline-of-christianity-continues-at-rapid-pace/.

[4] Canada's Changing Religious Landscape," *Pew Research Center*, June 27, 2013, https://www.pewforum.org/2013/06/27/canadas-changing-religious-landscape/.

[5] Chris Baynes, "Church of England staring at oblivion as just 2% of young Britons say they identify with it," *The Independent*, September 7, 2018, https://www.independent.co.uk/news/uk/home-news/church-england-uk-young-adults-identify-british-social-attitudes-a8527136.html.

[6] Jonathan Evans and Chris Baronavski, "How do European countries differ in religious commitment? Use our interactive map to find out," *Pew Research Center*, December 5, 2018, https://www.pewresearch.org/fact-tank/2018/12/05/how-do-european-countries-differ-in-religious-commitment/.

[7] Guy Stagg, *The Crossway* (London: Picador, 2018).

[8] Dave Whitson, "Episode 41: The Crossway," January 15, 2020, in *The Camino Podcast*, produced by Dave Whitson, https://soundcloud.com/user-939742370.

[9] Robert Putnam, *Bowling Alone: The Collapse and Revival of American Community* (New York City: Touchstone Books, 2001).

[10] Jesse Graham and Jonathan Haidt, "Beyond Beliefs: Religions Bind Individuals Into Moral Communities," *Personality and Social Psychology Review* 14, no. 1 (2010): 140-150, doi: 10.1177/1088868309353415.

[11] Arthur C. Brooks, *Gross National Happiness: Why Happiness Matters for America—and How We Can Get More of It* (New York City: Basic Books, 2008).

[12] Ed Diener and Martin E.P. Seligman, "Very Happy People," *Psychological Science* 13, no. 1 (2002): 81-84, doi: 10.1111/1467-9280.00415

[13] Steven Monsma, "Religion and Philanthropic Giving and Volunteering: Building Blocks for Civic Responsibility," *Interdisciplinary Journal of Research on Religion* 3, no. 1 (2007): 3-28.
[14] Michael Wolfe, *The Hadj: An American's Pilgrimage to Mecca* (New York City: Grove Press, 1998).
[15] Viktor Frankl, *Man's Search for Meaning* (New York City: Pocket Books, 1984).
[16] Sheldon Solomon, Jeff Greenberg, and Tom Pyszczynski, *Worm at the Core: On the Role of Death in Life* (New York City: Random House, 2015).
[17] Johann Hari, *Lost Connections: Uncovering the Real Causes of Depression—and Unexpected Solutions* (New York City: Bloomsbury, 2018).
[18] Mats Nilsson and Mekonnen Tesfahuney, "Performing the 'post-secular' in Santiago de Compostela," *Annals of Tourism Research* 57, no. 1 (2016): 18-30, doi: 10.1016/j.annals.2015.11.001.
[19] Paul Heelas and Linda Woodhead, *The Spiritual Revolution: Why Religion is Giving Way to Spirituality* (Hoboken, NJ: Wiley-Blackwell, 2005).
[20] Mats Nilsson, "Wanderers in the shadow of the sacred myth: pilgrims in the 21st century," *Social and Cultural Geography* 19, no. 1 (2018): 21-38, doi: 10.1080/14649365.2016.1249398.
[21] Suzanne Amaro, Angela Antunes, and Carla Henriques, "A closer look at Santiago de Compostela's pilgrims through the lens of motivations," *Tourism Management* 64, no. 1 (2018): 271-280, doi: 10.1016/j.tourman.2017.09.007.
[22] Robert Shepherd, Larry Yu, and Gu Huimin, "Tourism, heritage, and sacred space: Wutai Shan, China," *Journal of Heritage Tourism* 7, no. 2 (2012): 145-161, doi: 10.1080/1743873X.2011.637630.
[23] Xinzhong Yao, "Religious Belief and Practice in Urban China 1995-2005," *Journal of Contemporary Religion* 22, no. 2 (2007): 169-185, doi: 10.1080/13537900701331031.
[24] Tatjana Schnell and Sarah Pali, "Pilgrimage today: the meaning-making potential of ritual," *Mental Health, Religion & Culture* 16, no. 9 (2013): 887-902, doi: 10.1080/13674676.2013.766449.
[25] Deana L. Weibel, "Magnetism and Microwaves: Religion as Radiation," in *Religion and the Body: Modern Science and the Construction of Religious Meaning*, eds. David Cave and Rebecca Sachs Norris (Boston: Brill, 2012), 169-198, doi: 10.1163/9789004225343_010.
[26] Jill Dubisch and Michael Winkelman, eds., *Pilgrimage and Healing* (Tucson, AZ: University of Arizona Press, 2014).
[27] Dallen J. Timothy and Daniel H. Olsen, eds., *Tourism, Religion, & Spiritual Journeys* (New York City: Routledge, 2006).
[28] Mara W. Cohen Ioannides and Dimitri Ioannides, "Global Jewish tourism: Pilgrimages and remembrance," in *Tourism, Religion, & Spiritual Journeys*, eds. Dallen J. Timothy and Daniel H. Olsen (New York City: Routledge, 2006), 156-171.
[29] Dallen J. Timothy, "Tourism and the personal heritage experience," *Annals of Tourism Research* 34 (1997), 751–754.
[30] Lisbeth Mikaelsson, "Pilgrimage as post-secular therapy," *Post-Secular Religious Practices* 24, no. 1 (2012): 259-273, doi: 10.30674/scripta.67418.
[31] Kathryn Rountree, "Journeys to the Goddess: Pilgrimage and Tourism in the New Age," in *On the Road to Being There: Studies in Pilgrimage and Tourism in Late Modernity*, ed. William H. Swatos, Jr. (Boston: Brill, 2006), 33-60.

[32] Alice Warrender, *An Accidental Jubilee* (York: Stone Trough Books, 2012).
[33] P.A. Morris, "The effect of pilgrimage on anxiety, depression and religious attitude," *Psychological Medicine* 12, no. 1 (1982): 291-294, doi: 10.1017/S0033291700046626.

Conclusion

[1] Dave Whitson, "Episode 50: Pilgrimage and Peace-Building," January 2, 2021, in *The Camino Podcast*, produced by Dave Whitson, https://soundcloud.com/user-939742370
[2] Ian McIntosh, *Pilgrimage: Walking to Peace, Walking for Change* (Xlibris, 2020).
[3] John Hornblow and Jenny Boyack, "Pilgrimages of Transformation and Reconciliation: Māori and Pākehā Walking Together in Aotearoa New Zealand," in *The Many Voices of Pilgrimage and Reconciliation,* ed. Ian S. McIntosh (Boston: CABI, 2017).
[4] Dave Whitson, "Episode 51: Pilgrimage, Reconciliation, and Decolonization," January 6, 2021, in *The Camino Podcast*, produced by Dave Whitson, https://soundcloud.com/user-939742370
[5] James K. Sebenius, Kimberlyn Leary, and Joshua N. Weiss, "Negotiating the Path of Abraham," *Harvard Business School* Case N9-912-017, https://www.homeworkforyou.com/static_media/uploadedfiles/API%20HBS%20Case%20Dec%202011.pdf.
[6] William Ury, "The walk from 'no' to 'yes,'" *TED*, October 2010, video, https://www.ted.com/talks/william_ury_the_walk_from_no_to_yes?language=en.
[7] Brian Mockenhaupt, "Searching for Peace on the West Bank's Abraham Path," *Backpacker*, last updated February 14, 2017, https://www.backpacker.com/stories/searching-for-peace-on-the-west-banks-abraham-path.
[8] P.C. Stern and T. Dietz, "The Value Basis of Environmental Concern," Journal of Social Issues, 50 (1994): 65–84.
[9] P. Wesley Schultz, "Empathizing With Nature: The Effects of Perspective Taking on Concern for Environmental Issues," Journal of Social Issues 56, 3 (2000): 391-406.
[10] Cynthia McPherson Frantz and F. Stephan Mayer, "The Importance of Connection to Nature in Assessing Environmental Education Programs," *Studies in Educational Evaluation*, 41 (2014): 85-89.
[11] Mary Lee Nolan and Sidney Nolan, Christian Pilgrimage in Modern Western Europe (Chapel Hill: University of North Carolina Press, 1989).
[12] Rosie Scammell, "Ex-climate negotiator hopes for 'miracle' on people's pilgrimage," *The Guardian*, September 30, 2015, https://www.theguardian.com/environment/2015/sep/30/ex-climate-negotiator-peoples-pilgrimage-pope-francis-yeb-sano-walk-rome-paris.
[13] Cole Mellino, "Yeb Saño Embarks on 930-Mile Walk From Rome to Paris Demanding World Leaders Take Climate Action," *EcoWatch*, October 1, 2015,

https://www.ecowatch.com/yeb-sano-embarks-on-930-mile-walk-from-rome-to-paris-demanding-world-l-1882105784.html

[14] "The Journey Continues," *Climate Pilgrimage*, http://climatepilgrimage.com/the-journey-continues/.

[15] David L. Chandler, "Study: Climate change could pose danger for Muslim pilgrimage," *MIT* News, August 22, 2019, https://news.mit.edu/2019/climate-muslim-hajj-0822.

[16] Shaia, *Returning from Camino*.

[17] Dave Whitson, "Episode 34: How Strange It Will Be To Come Home," December 8, 2019, in *The Camino Podcast*, produced by Dave Whitson, https://soundcloud.com/user-939742370.

[18] Dave Whitson, "Episode 37: Phil Cousineau's Art of Pilgrimage," December 18, 2019, in *The Camino Podcast*, produced by Dave Whitson, https://soundcloud.com/user-939742370.